ST. MARY'S UNIVERSITY COI   ARY
A COLLEGE OF THE QUEENS UNIVI

Tel. 028 90
Web site ww
email: lib   **for Unity Amid Diversity**

STRIVING FOR UNITY AMID DIVERSITY

Mark D. Lowery

TWENTY-THIRD PUBLICATIONS
Mystic, Connecticut

Twenty-Third Publications
P.O. Box 180
Mystic, CT 06355
(203) 536-2611

Library of Congress Catalog Card Number 85-51087
ISBN 0-89622-274-8

Edited by Gwen Costello
Designed by Andrea Star

FOREWORD

I am pleased to write a foreword to Mark Lowery's book, *Ecumenism: Striving for Unity Amid Diversity*. Lowery's study, I believe, represents a real achievement in several respects, and I hope that those who read and use it will agree. This book, first of all, presents a sound, succinct, and highly readable Catholic approach to ecumenical doctrine and the church's perspective on contemporary ecumenical relations. It is, thus, a publication that will advance a general understanding to all who are interested in learning about the relationship between Catholicism and the faith traditions of other Christians who have, for a variety of unfortunate reasons, become separated through the centuries. Lowery's book, moreover, is a collaborative effort in the best sense of the term and thus bears the imprint of a number of contributors who have helped make its appearance a reality.

This book was conceived in May 1981 at a meeting of the education committee of the Ecumenical and Interfaith Commission of the Archdiocese of Milwaukee. For several months, the committee's members had engaged in a continuing discussion as to how we might best reach larger numbers of Catholics in our community to provide them with intellectually sound, readily absorbable and useful knowledge about ecumenism. We realized that for many Catholics ecumenism was, and remains, a low priority in their faith experience while for others it was, and is, a source of some disquiet. But most Catholics, the committee felt, were simply ambivalent about ecumenism. They seemed not interested in discussing it in a systematic fashion, even though, in a practical sense, ecumenical contacts are taking place increasingly as Christians deal with one another's values in our communities, schools, places of work, and through marriage. This ambivalence, we concluded, was due at least in part to a lack of knowledge of the subject. One way in which this problem could be dealt with was, we felt, through the development of educational programs designed to meet the needs of interested parish members and teachers.

We realized, however, that if such programs were to be put into operation, a solid and up-to-date introduction to ecumenism was needed (as well as guidelines for reading about it). After searching without success to find such materials already in print, we decided to develop our own.

For their faithful support of this project from the start, let me express my gratitude to the members of the Ecumenical and Interfaith Commission and its educational committee. All of us, of course, appreciate the help given by the editorial staff of Twenty-Third Publications as well. Let me thank above all, Mark Lowery, who has worked so hard on this project and who has so patiently and so pleasantly accepted our suggestions, some useful, some impractical, some redundant, in the best spirit. (There are, after all, burdens as well as benefits connected with collaboration!) Mark has, in the end, made a significant contribution of his talents. No doubt his work will serve to enrich the lives of many with a better understanding of the relationship between our Roman Catholic tradition and the tradition of our fellow Christians.

Only time will tell how successful our effort to build knowledge, understanding, and respect in the area of ecumenism will ultimately be. We cannot foretell the future, but we can and have done something tangible and constructive, I am proud to say, in supporting this publication to advance the cause of ecumenism. That is something of real value.

Donald E. Pienkos, Ph.D.
University of Wisconsin at Milwaukee
Chairman, Education Committee
Ecumenical and Interfaith Commission
The Archdiocese of Milwaukee

PREFACE

Several deeply held convictions lie at the heart of this book about ecumenism. First, in order for Christianity to remain a credible and transforming force in the modern world, Christians on all sides must direct their efforts toward genuine unity. I am convinced that the beginnings of the ecumenical spirit that must pervade our lives lie in a willingness to abandon polemical attitudes toward one another. Second, this fresh attitude of openness has nothing to do with abandoning one's own distinctive set of beliefs, but rather involves a reshaping of the way in which those beliefs are held. They are not weapons to be used against one another, but instead form the matrix for dialogue. The church of the future by no means can or should strive for uniformity of belief, but rather unity amid diversity. Third, the evolution of a truly ecumenical Christianity must be developed among individuals who work together at the local, grassroots level. The scholarship of theologians and the leadership of official church leaders is empty and lifeless otherwise.

It may benefit the reader to take a glimpse at some of the experiences that have led me to these convictions. I imagine that you will, perhaps, identify with some of them, giving us a common ground on which to begin our journey. Three experiences stand out in my mind. The first involves the ordinary day-to-day living in a neighborhood. In the midst of the casual small talk, the children playing together, helping each other with some project or other, working through a disagreement, sharing happy occasions—through all this, simple but beautiful bonds are formed. And yet there is the nagging suspicion that these bonds could be all the more profound if we were somehow more unified as regards our faith, if we felt at ease rather than slightly suspicious in this most important dimension of our lives.

A second experience is closely related to this. While making the short trip to my own parish on Sundays, a certain sadness would overtake me as I realized that so many people in my city were making their own trips to other churches. We were all doing the same thing, rooted in a common instinct to worship God, but in a sense we were doing it without harmony. Over a period of several months, I took opportunities to visit and worship at the churches of each tradition discussed in the chapters to follow.

A third experience had to do with social action. Over the years I had worked with people from diverse traditions to promote, in however small a way, the causes of peace and justice in our society and in our world. While working to provide food, shelter, and clothing to those in need, I felt the potential for unity that existed beneath our divisions.

I had the fourth and final experience while doing doctoral work in a theology department. This department brought together students and professors from a variety of traditions. Again I thought, if only we could explore the unity beneath our divisions! All of these experiences convinced me that we could only stand to become enriched by finding new ways to tap the resources of our faith with an ecumenical attitude.

This text is meant to facilitate the task of developing that attitude. As such, it is but a springboard, so to speak, for study groups in a variety of contexts to use in pursuing ecumenical theology and action. The book invites you to do the essential work of ecumenism—getting involved with people of other traditions. In an attempt to provide you with a starting point for your own endeavors, I have tried to pave a "middle way" between a too scholarly account that would remain inaccessible to the general reader, and a too superficial treatment that would almost insult the intelligence of an educated Catholic layperson. Thus, theologians will invariably find the text too simplified at times, with perhaps some inexcusable omissions. On the other hand, someone looking for a few evenings of easy reading will find something more challenging here. Extensive footnotes have been avoided to make for smoother reading. A bibliography is included for those wishing to pursue certain themes in more depth. All works referred to in the text, in shortened form, are found in this bibliography.

The idea for this book originated among members of the Ecumenical and Interfaith Commission of the Archdiocese of Milwaukee who saw the need for a single text that gathered the key issues and concerns of ecumenism as seen through Roman Catholic eyes. It was indeed a privilege to be invited to write the main body of the text, and I wish to thank the many people whose dedication to ecumenism helped bring the project to fruition. Special thanks are due to Sister Maureen Hopkins, S.D.S., the former coordinator of the Ecumenical and Interfaith Commission; Dr. Donald Pienkos of the University of Wisconsin at Milwaukee, chairman of the Education Committee of the Commission; Archbishop Rembert G. Weakland of the Milwaukee Archdiocese, who supported the project throughout; Robert O'Hara Schmitt, who provided valuable editing work; Mark Kemmeter, Maureen Gallagher, and Joan DeMerchant, who enhanced the methodology of the text; Bert Mulroy, who succeeded Sr. Maureen Hopkins as coordinator, for his help in completing the tasks connected with the book's eventual appearance; and finally, gracious thanks to Dr. Paul Misner of Marquette University for his invaluable scholarly assistance throughout the writing of the book.

ACKNOWLEDGMENTS

Maureen Gallagher, Coordinator of the Adult
and Family Ministry Office
The Archdiocese of Milwaukee.

Joan De Merchant, Adult and Family Ministry Office
The Archdiocese of Milwaukee.

Mark Kemmeter, Ecumenical and Interfaith Commission
The Archdiocese of Milwaukee

Bert Mulroy, Coordinator of the Ecumenical
and Interfaith Office
The Archdiocese of Milwaukee.

Ruth Bartz, Script Typist, Ecumenical and Interfaith Office
The Archdiocese of Milwaukee.

Methodological Suggestions

1.   This book is meant to be used as a basic guide in a small discussion group context of adults, advanced high school students, or college students. Of course, it may be appropriate in other contexts as well, including private reading. The text is meant to be self-sufficient for a group leader who does not have the time or resources to gather materials for a discussion group on ecumenism.

2.   As mentioned in the introduction, a text alone is an inadequate and rather lifeless tool. Ecumenical education must involve members of the various traditions in order to be truly effective. Not only must we become acquainted with one another's history, faith, and religious life, but we must also become acquainted with one another personally. Here are four practical ways to do this:

a)   Organize the small group in such a way that all members of the group attend the services of the various traditions discussed. This may be done either before or after the group has met to discuss a particular tradition. The group will be anxious to discuss their experience and reactions, and therefore, this is an excellent way of assuring lively discussion within the group. Be sure to present the material on intercommunion from Chapter Six prior to attending any services together.

b)   It would be profitable to invite a pastor, leader, or knowledgeable representative of each tradition to attend discussions in the small group meetings. The leader can search out such people on their own or perhaps get assistance from the diocesan Office of Ecumenism. The invited guest could either lead the group discussion, give a short presentation, or be available in a more casual way to share ideas and answer questions.

c)   The leader need not feel restricted to inviting just one person from a tradition. There may be situations in which a number of lay people from a congregation could be invited to join the discussion.

d)   Encourage the members of the study group to take advantage of ecumenical opportunities "right in their own backyard." For example, most people have neighbors or friends of different traditions who would be happy to discuss their common faith traditions.

3.   Look for opportunities in which the small group can reach out to encourage ecumenical activity for a wider group within the parish. Suggestions for such activity can be found in Chapter Five. It is at this point that a small group may want to begin planning a larger parish project, such as an ecumenical worship service.

4.   A good portion of the book deals with the historical background of the various traditions considered. The reasons for this are outlined in "step three" of the ecumenical method. Very often people have a negative attitude toward the study of history. However, it is ignorance of history that is responsible for so many biases and difficulties people have in understanding others. Therefore, it is important to present the historical material in this positive light.

5.   As pointed out in Chapter One, the Documents of Vatican II are a resource of inestimable value to this ecumenical endeavor. It is assumed that the leader should have enough familiarity with these documents to make good use of them throughout the time the small group meets. Depending on the time available, it may be good to work through parts of certain documents together.

6.   There is a wide variety of "interesting facts" about the various traditions that are intentionally not covered in this text. Such facts, such as demographic figures and geographical locations, can be found in any almanac-style treatment of the churches, some of which are listed in the bibliography. One suggestion is to have different members of the group look up such facts and present them at the respective meetings.

CONTENTS

Foreword *(by Dr. Donald E. Pienkos)*   v

Preface   vii

Acknowledgments   xi

Methodological Suggestions   xiii

CHAPTER ONE
An Ecumenical Perspective   1

CHAPTER TWO
A History of Ecumenism   23

CHAPTER THREE
Early Christianity   39

CHAPTER FOUR
The Orthodox Tradition   48

CHAPTER FIVE
The Lutheran Tradition   64

CHAPTER SIX
Anglicanism/The Episcopal Church   86

CHAPTER SEVEN
The Presbyterian/Reformed Tradition   109

CHAPTER EIGHT
   The Methodist Tradition   132

CHAPTER NINE
   The Evangelicals   153

Conclusion *(by Brother Jeffrey Gros, F.S.C.)*   169

Annotated Bibliography   173

ECUMENISM: Striving for Unity Amid Diversity

CHAPTER ONE

An
Ecumenical
Perspective

Think of the neighborhood you live in or, for that matter, think about any American neighborhood. Within several miles of your home, a number of different churches can probably be found. You go to your own Catholic church on Sundays, and you see other people going to other churches. When you see these other people, you probably do not feel anger and bitterness. Since the Second Vatican Council in the early 1960s, most of the animosity that once existed between Catholics and non-Catholics has subsided. Perhaps you have heard stories from the past about such animosity and even outright hostility. In light of those past attitudes, we have come a long way, and we can be rightfully proud of the progress we've made in our relations with other churches.

During the decade or so following the council, there was a good deal of popular enthusiasm for ecumenical endeavors. Many imagined that real unity was right around the corner. Then, as the task proved to be more difficult than imagined, much of the initial enthusiasm subsided. We had reached a comfortable plateau in which we were "good neighbors." Now, since there is no outright hostility between us to speak of, why

1

bother to go any further toward unity? Why embark on this study of ecumenism?

As we look at the American religious scene, we find that there are over 40 different denominational groups, all falling under the general heading of Christianity. And then, with this diversity in mind, we read these words of Jesus in the Gospel of John:

> I pray...that all may be one as you, Father, are in me, and I in you. I pray that they may be one in us, that the world may believe that you sent me. I have given them the glory you gave me that they may be one, as we are one—I living in them, you living in me—that their unity may be complete (17:20-23).

Although all the members of Christian denominations read about this desire of Jesus, how much energy do we put forth practicing it? Can we really be satisfied with our tidy arrangement of various communions existing side by side, without anger and animosity, but also without genuine understanding and dialogue? The words that, perhaps, best describe the present state of affairs are "stumbling blocks." Christian disunity is a stumbling block, a hindrance, for several different groups of people in today's world.

Disunity as a Stumbling Block   There are four major groups of people who suffer because of disunity. First, many people today have been so affected by the secularism within our culture that they no longer allow room in their lives for a religious dimension. Christianity, above all, must give witness to the existence of a gracious God who satisfies our hunger for a truly meaningful and human existence. But the witness given is so fragmented and disunified that Christianity seems to be missing its chance to be a sign through which the secularized world may come to believe. According to the Decree on Ecumenism from Vatican II, "Without doubt, this discord openly contradicts the will of Christ, provides a stumbling block to the world, and inflicts damage on the most holy cause of proclaiming the good news to every creature" (art. 1).

Second, there are many people who do feel a genuine need for a transcendant dimension in their lives, something beyond them that might shed light on the deep mysteries of their existence. But they find the institutionalized forms of Christianity wanting because of the fragmentation and quarrelling that appear from the outside to be so needless and unconstructive. Young people especially seem negatively affected by the disunity that exists among the followers of Jesus. In turn, many reach for any number of other "solutions" that promise some structure and meaning amid a complex, rapidly changing culture.

Third, Christian disunity is also a stumbling block for those already within the various Christian communions. We are all the poorer for our lack of cohesiveness and openness, for our inability to follow through on Jesus' desire for unity among his followers. As we shall discover in the chapters to come, we end up shutting ourselves off from the many riches within each other's traditions that have the potential to enhance and broaden our own perspective.

Finally, Christian unity is in fact a hindrance for all of humanity. In a world characterized by disunity and fragmentation on so many fronts, Christianity ought to act as the "conscience" of the modern world, a reminder, a home where peace and unity can be found. According to the Decree on Ecumenism, "What has revealed the love of God among us is that the only begotten Son of God has been sent by the Father into the world, so that, being made man, the Son might by his redemption of the entire human race give new life to it and unify it" (art. 2). Thus, ideal as it may sound, God desires the entire human family to be peacefully unified. Christ meant for his church to be a sign of such unity.

We are on the verge of completing the second millenium— in a short time, the year 2000 will have arrived. On the first day of that year, what will Christianity look like? If it looks like it does right now, it will be embarrassing and frightening to realize that in the year 1000, Christianity was more unified than it is now. After 2000 years, shouldn't we be able to present to the world a more cohesive and unified Christianity?*

---

*This "examination of conscience" is from Raymond Brown, *The Critical Meaning of the Bible.* p. 108.

If this is to happen, a real change of heart, or conversion, needs to take place within us. There must be a sense of pain over our divisions and a genuine desire to work actively for a more unified Christianity. The question is how precisely do we go about doing this?

Steps for Ecumenism   We are proposing a very concrete method for ecumenism. It consists of the seven basic steps or stages listed here, which shall be outlined in the remaining sections of this chapter and then built upon as we move through the book.

1. Recognize that separation exists among Christian denominations.
2. Experience conversion rooted in openness and loyalty.
3. Understand history.
4. Understand the present situation.
5. Discover a common tradition.
6. Recognize and appreciate diverse traditions.
7. Set a goal for the future.

1. Recognition

The first of these steps we have in fact just been covering: the basic recognition that separation exists among those who all claim to be members of Christ's true church and a basic interest in discovering what might be done about it. As the Decree on Ecumenism states, "This very concern already reveals to some extent the bond of brotherhood existing among all Christians, and it leads toward that full and perfect unity which God lovingly desires" (art. 5). With this, we can move on to step two.

2. Conversion and Openness

In his introductory commentary to the Decree on Ecumenism, Walter Abbott indicates that conversion is at the root or foundation of all ecumenical activity:

> The council moves into action in this contrite spirit: all have an obligation to pray and work for the restoration of unity;

all are called to dialogue according to their ability; all are called to further common efforts...in prayer and social action. These are not mere words and plans. This is a call to action. And one is always to remember the essential thing: change of heart.

What precisely is this change of heart, or conversion, that is the ground and springboard, the one "essential thing," in our quest for unity?

There are two interrelated aspects to this conversion. First, sound ecumenism presupposes an attitude of genuine openness to other traditions. Many Catholics today find this openness to be a spontaneous attitude within them. On the other hand, many other Catholics are understandably hesitant about such openness, convinced it will threaten and diminish the uniquely Catholic identity. A primary thesis in this book is that good ecumenical theology allows for, and in fact demands, both an attitude of openness to others and a strong sense of loyalty to one's own tradition. These two aspects or attitudes can and must exist in a creative tension with each other; they are, in fact, complementary and can enhance one another. This complementary will unfold in the chapters to follow. Thus a two-fold conversion is at work in step two of our method. One becomes a) more open to others and b) more in touch with and more faithful to one's unique Catholic tradition.

The documents of Vatican II offer a brilliant and inspiring source for this balanced, two-pronged approach. They form the basis of the underlying theology in this book. Before moving on to step three, let's introduce and clarify these two attitudes in light of Vatican II.

We have all had the experience in our relationships with other people of closing ourselves off from them, not wanting to talk and not wanting to listen. If the relationship is to continue, we know that some change must eventually take place in which we open up to each other once again. In our relations with other churches, the same dynamic is at work. In the past, we have been close-minded toward them, convinced that we as Catholics are right and they are wrong. After all, what good does it do to listen to someone whom you already know is wrong?

If we are to achieve further unity in Christianity, we must free ourselves from our defensive tendencies; we must learn to listen to one another and dialogue with one another. Dialogue is an activity Pope John Paul II has consistently encouraged. To dialogue means coming to the other with an openness and a willingness to be changed, to be enriched. We cannot be like the person who will only talk about himself or herself, never showing an interest in the other, never asking a question, and thus only demonstrating insecurity. As Catholics, a flawed part of the beautiful tradition we inherit is a defensive attitude. Such an attitude causes us to show interest in the beliefs of others only insofar as we might be able to convert him. We have built up a vast array of defense mechanisms throughout the past centuries: "We are right and they are wrong"; "There will be division until they see the light and return to the one true fold"; "Salvation is only available within the Catholic Church—all others are excluded"; "The Protestants have made all the mistakes in the past—the disunity is all their fault."

At Vatican II, a tremendous change of attitude occurred, and a successful effort was made to abandon these defense mechanisms. We find a reevaluation of the whole nature of the church itself in the Dogmatic Constitution on the Church. This document is the grounding point or foundation of the other fifteen documents, all of which further develop its major themes. While we will look to this primary document for evidence of the attitudinal shift made at the council, we will also find of special interest the Decree on Ecumenism, already quoted several times. We will summarize here three aspects of the richness of Vatican II's new perspective.

The Church as Mystery   The very title of the opening chapter of the Constitution on the Church, "The Mystery of the Church," signals a profound change and marks a new era in the history of Catholicism. Instead of being a static institution that is set and defined once and for all, the church is identified with much more dynamism and openness as a mystery. This has a myriad of implications, to which we shall refer often. Pope Paul VI, in an opening address to the council, suggests the primary implication: "The church is a mystery. It is a reality imbued with the hidden presence of God. It lies, therefore, within the very nature of the church to be always open to new and greater exploration" (Abbott, p.14). Two areas in which such explorations have taken place are biblical studies and the liturgy. Both are closely connected with ecumenism as Catholics and non-Catholics learn much from each other.

The Church as Catholic   This leads us to a second facet of Vatican II's new perspective. The word "catholic" means universal, and implies a willingness to embrace all truth, wherever it may be found. In its willingness to openly explore, the council set an unprecedented universal and ecumenical tone for the church. The council itself has been termed an adventure in ecumenical cooperation; Protestant, Anglican, and Orthodox representatives were present at the sessions, and their responses are published in the collection of documents. There is a marked sense of abandoning the so-called "ghetto" or "fortress" mentality of the past decades in which the church was often seen as a private sect holding off against the onslaught of the world in favor of a much more open attitude.

The Church as a Pilgrim   The new image of the church was summarized at the council with the term "pilgrim church," echoing the theme of exploration and openness. As a pilgrim church, we have not yet arrived at our full perfection. On her journey, the church must travel through many varied cultures and epochs; inevitably, mistakes will be made. Thus, we are constantly in need of reform and renewal: "Christ summons the church, as she goes her pilgrim way, to that continual reformation of which she always has need, insofar as she is an institution of men here on earth" (Decree on Ecumenism, art. 5). This is what Pope John XXIII meant by focusing on the Italian word *aggiornamento,* which means revitalization, renewal, and updating. The church had recovered the basic principle underlying the Protestant Reformation that the church, by its very nature, must always be open to reform.

We all know that it takes a great deal of courage to admit having made a mistake. Often such an admission is what re-kindles a friendship. One of the real merits of the Decree on Ecumenism was its admission that in the past both sides made mistakes, not just the Protestants, Anglicans, and Orthodox (art. 3). We will be examining some of those historical mistakes in future chapters.

There is a good deal of responsibility that comes with being a member of a pilgrim church. Good ecumenical inten-tions must be grounded by the sound insights and skills that come from careful inquiry. As the Decree on Ecumenism states:

> We must come to understand the outlook of our separated brethren. Study is absolutely required for this, and should be pursued with fidelity to truth and in a spirit of good will.... Catholics need to acquire a more adequate understanding of the distinctive doctrines of our separated brethren, as well as of their history, spiritual and liturgical life, their religious psychology and cultural background (art. 9).

It is a challenge that the Council offers to every Catholic. In fact, an entire document, the Decree on the Apostolate of the Laity, asks every member of the church to become respon-sibly involved. An introductory comment to this decree sum-marizes the point succinctly:

> Indeed, the renewal of the church, called for by the documents of the Council, depends in great part on a laity that fully under-stands not only these documents but also their own co-respon-sibility for the mission of Christ in the church and in the world. (Martin H. Work in Abbott, p. 486).

Loyalty and Commitment   The type of openness de-scribed above could be termed an informed, cautious open-ness. There is a type of openness, however, that can be carried to an extreme, with detrimental effects. This is an "all out" openness that says "everybody's right," "we're all really the same," or "one is just as good as the other." The problem with such an attitude is that it pays as little attention to the dis-tinctive beliefs of other Christians as the "closed-off" attitude does. This leads us to an idea that stands in tension with the idea of openness: loyalty to one's own position and tradition. As the Decree on Ecumenism warns, we must

> abstain from any superficiality or imprudent zeal, for these can cause harm to true progress toward unity. (Our) ecumenical activity must not be other than fully and sincerely Catholic, that is, loyal to the truth we have received from the apostles and the Fathers, and in harmony with the faith that the Catholic Church has always professed, and at the same time tending toward that fullness with which our Lord wants his body to be endowed in the course of time (art. 24).

In a response to the Decree, it was wisely written, "When we are trying to see things through the eyes of another, we may be tempted to be so amiable that our differences are obscured or blurred. For genuine and fruitful dialogue, candor is as essential as respect" (Samuel McCrea Cavert).

We have two values, then, that stand in tension with each other. Our process of ecumenical conversion must take place in two directions simultaneously: on the one hand, a change of heart must take place through which we become genuinely more open to other traditions, with a willingness to allow our own tradition to be transformed. But on the other hand, in loyalty to our own cherished historical identity as Roman Catholics, we want to be sure to preserve our rich heritage. We must be both open and loyal; we must both transform and preserve. We have centuries of splendid tradition behind us that we cannot afford to lose; a change of heart must take place in which a certain thirst is instilled within us for this tradition, beckoning us to become more in touch with it, more knowledgeable about it, and more faithfully committed to it. But, as mentioned earlier, we are a pilgrim church with a mission not yet completed, so transformation and adaptation must always be part of the life of our church. In light of this two-pronged conversion, the ecumenical challenge is analogous to walking a tightrope. It is a difficult though rewarding task that cannot be accomplished unless the rope is taut, with tension provided by both sides to keep a healthy balance.

As we have pointed out, good intentions alone, however sincere, are thoroughly inadequate for sound ecumenical endeavors. We have plenty of "ecu-maniacs" running around all set to start one big super-church, who have no sensitivity at all to the complexity of the ecumenical endeavor. They lack thorough knowledge about the Christian tradition in all its facets. The one thing that must ground healthy ecumenism is education.

We must always be in the process of becoming more educated ourselves. A Catholic theologian, Bernard Lonergan, tells us that within each of us is a pure and unrestricted desire to know. We have the capacity to ask unending questions about all of reality and search out the answers. Our own unending education must involve both of the aspects under discussion here. To begin with, we want to become more acquainted with our own Catholic tradition. As we acquaint ourselves with the richness of our own tradition, however, there is the awareness that it does not exist in a vacuum throughout history; rather, it exists alongside the many other Christian traditions that have developed in their own right among those separated from Catholicism. We must also develop an openness toward other traditions that can broaden our own horizons. And so, our own education can include both the aspect of preserving our own heritage and the aspect of possible transformation with the final goal of Christian unity.

3.   An Understanding of History

We have seen that the method for ecumenism in step one is a basic realization that disunity exists and is harmful, and step two involves recognizing the need for a change of heart toward those separated from us. How can this change of heart, resulting in a genuine openness toward other traditions, begin to take place? A short story will help answer this question. As you read, try to think of an experience you have had that might be analogous to the experience of the people in the story.

You are teaching or supervising a group of young people, and there is one youngster whom you instinctively dislike. You realize that aspects of his personality disturb you; he isn't as spontaneous as the others, he doesn't seem interested in contributing to the group, and you find his mannerisms annoying.

You are prejudiced against him. It's not an easy feeling to get rid of. You don't treat him like the other members of the group; in many subtle ways you tend to ignore him because he just isn't "normal." Then one evening his mother stops to pick him up, and you find yourself in conversation with her. After some small talk, she begins telling you about her family. She refers to her husband, from whom she separated several years earlier. She talks about how not living with their father has influenced the children, how they don't seem the same anymore. She mentions that her son in your group seems to have taken it the hardest; after his father left, he began having difficulties getting along with his friends.

During the conversation, you have been discovering the history of the boy you had disliked. As you discover that history, you begin to understand where he has come from and you gain insight into his appearing less "normal" than the other members of your class. You see why he has developed habits that keep him from relating easily to other people. Now that you know his history, your attitude changes. You realize that perhaps he needs your sensitivity, more than the other members of the group. A conversion, a change of heart, has taken place. It began with your understanding of his past.

In this book, we will use an analogous approach. Step three in our ecumenical process occurs in two phases. 1) What separated us historically? 2) What still separates us?

When we look to those separated from us, we will begin by asking ourselves how the separation occurred in the first place. Just as conversion occurred in the story above, once there was an understanding of the boy's history, so, too, in ecumenism a great deal of conversion and healing can take place when we start to understand the underlying historical reasons behind our separation. In the story, knowing the boy's history led to a greater appreciation and sensitivity toward him. The prejudice vanished. Likewise, our openness toward non-Catholics can be furthered as we develop a sense of history. Our understandings and misconceptions about what is happening now can be corrected by insight into the original historical context from which our division began. We will be looking to two main eras in history: first, the eleventh century, during which Christianity split into two main divisions, East and West; and second, the time of the Protestant Reformation during the sixteenth century.

There exists a startling complexity to the many divisions of Christianity. The divisions were caused not simply by certain groups disagreeing about religious ideas and practices, but also by a vast interplay of many factors: theological, political, socio-economic, psychological. Added to this intricate interplay was the fact that opposing parties were simply unwilling to openly dialogue with each other.

4. Understand the Present Situation

Consider another short story that, by use of analogy, summarizes the previous step and also outlines the next step for us. Imagine that you have just moved into a new neighborhood. To your dismay you discover that your neighbors next door have a dog that stays outside and habitually barks loudly during the early morning hours. While your neighbors sleep right through it, you find it quite irritating and can't get used to it at all. Eventually, you stop over at the neighbor's to discuss the situation; you end up expressing some anger at them. Offended, the neighbors react defensively. An argument ensues, and you part in bitterness.

As it turns out, this episode is the beginning of long years of mutual tension. Other things happen that seem to fuel the disagreement more and more. Eventually, a certain apathy over the situation settles in and you both simply ignore each other. Then one day you begin to reflect on the whole chain of events. The dog died long ago, and the immaturity once displayed on both sides has been outgrown. You begin to realize and admit that you made a lot of mistakes. Times have now changed; the original cause of the disunity, the original context of it, is gone. And you, too, have changed with the times. Nonetheless, the disunity still exists, but now for no good reason. The discomfort, built up layer upon layer over the years, is now no easy thing to remove.

At this point, you would like to patch things up, but you feel quite awkward taking a first step. Finally, you are motivated by a tragedy in your neighbor's lives. They obviously need a lot of support, and this is no time to continue years of quarrelling. A reconciliation finally takes place. You are still different people with different outlooks; you're not about to move in together! But you are ready to be open to each other and to work together in a time of crisis.

This analogy limps, as do all analogies, but perhaps it will help to clarify this aspect of our ecumenical method. In step three, we recognized the original historical context within which our disagreements began. Step four is like that day when you started thinking about the present, and realized that there was no longer a reason to quarrel. While step three was a journey to the past, step four is a close look at the present, in which we realize that we are in a new situation. History changed. The Renaissance is long gone; church/state relations have taken a turnaround; the Age of Enlightenment has occurred, and we are in the midst of a scientific revolution; the church is not the same church it was in the late middle ages.

The disagreements, the discomfort, the hesitancy to talk, and the strangeness still exist. But their original cause and context don't. We are in a new situation, a new cultural epoch. And this new epoch brings with it new needs to be met by Christianity. As we said earlier, a crucial need in a new, secularized culture is to present as cohesive as possible a witness to the Christian vision of God. Mutual support is needed. We will, of course, remain unique and different. But we must be willing to work together in a time of crisis.

5. A Common Tradition

Imagine the experience of a family in which the children have grown up and gone their separate ways. They no longer live in the same city; different careers and different lifestyles make each family member quite distinctive. As everyone settles down, it becomes more and more difficult to get together and keep in close touch. Yet, at special times of the year—Christmas, for example—the whole family is drawn together at least for a few days. Although there is a great deal of diversity

among all the family members, a common bond is felt, a
genuine feeling of togetherness. What causes this bond?
    Perhaps it is that everyone has returned to their common
roots, to the home where they grew up together. Although
each person has developed a distinctive set of values, there
exists the recognition that everyone shares a common set of
values handed down by the parents (e.g. always doing their
best, respecting others, acknowledging God, etc.) And there
is the recognition that everyone still takes delight in certain
basic traditions that reach back to childhood (decorating a tree,
celebrating Midnight Mass, a distinctive family meal, etc.).
It is this sense of common roots that will forever make all of
the distinctive individuals still one family.
    In step five of our ecumenical method, there is an analo-
gous recognition. We saw in step four that it no longer makes
sense to remain alienated. Now we see that reconciliation begins
when we reach far back in history to our common roots, our
common values, our common tradition. What is the common
tradition we all share as Christians? We can summarize it here
in four main points.

Our Tradition Begins in Judaism   Our common tradition begins in Judaism, the self revelation of God to the Israelite
people. Five hallmarks of the Israelite experience that we can
all acknowledge include: the emergence of monotheism where
one true God can be freely worshipped; the belief that God
created the world with meaning and purpose (which is the
essential meaning of the first creation story of Genesis); the
knowledge of the ultimate gift of freedom with which God
endowed all of humanity; the understanding of God as an
absolute mystery (as reflected especially in Exodus 3; Psalm
39, and Isaiah 55); the mysterious paradox that God is transcendent and immanent at the same time, that is to say, a
mystery beyond us yet close to us, intimately involved in
human life and human history.
    The God of the Israelites is a God who works in and
through the forces of history. Thus, history has meaning and
purpose, despite all indications to the contrary. It is not an
endless cycle of good and evil headed nowhere. Rather, God

has a plan for creation. It is headed toward the messianic kingdom, which Christians see as the second coming of Christ. These five points serve to highlight the legacy of the Israelites, a foundation that all Christians share in common. Also, this common legacy is what allows Christians to have healthy interfaith relations with modern-day Jews.

Jesus Christ, the Fullness of Revelation   The focal point of our common tradition is, of course, the self-revelation of God in Jesus Christ, who is "the light of the world, from whom we go forth, through whom we live, and toward whom our journey leads us" (ibid., art. 3). Jesus is Emmanuel, God-with-us. As such, he is the ultimate way in which our transcendent God expresses immanence—in our midst, within history. A highlight of our common tradition is the sharing of the eucharist in which we proclaim Jesus' death and resurrection, and together, look ahead to his second coming, the parousia. At many points in the chapters to follow, we will elaborate on our common Christological tradition.

Sacred Scriptures   The collective experiences of the Israelites and the early Christians are recorded in the sacred Scriptures. We all share the common belief that the Bible is inspired by God, that God speaks to us therein in a special and definitive way. The Bible is an amazingly complex work, and it therefore lends itself to a myriad of interpretations. Nonetheless, we can all look to it as a common source from which our diverse traditions flow, a foundation on which they are built.

The leaders of the Jewish and Christian communities had many writings available to them, and they only chose certain ones to be part of what we call the canon (for example, there was quite a variety of gospels written out of which the four we are familiar with were chosen). When we say these writings are canonical, we are claiming that they are, in fact, inspired and applicable for all time, and that those who chose them did so under the guidance of the Holy Spirit. The canon of Sacred Scripture thus forms a definitive part of our common tradition.

Belief in the Early Church   Finally, we share in common the belief that the early apostles and Fathers of the church taught the truths of Christianity in an authoritative and reliable fashion. They were responsible for guiding the early church through its transition from a small Jewish sect to an established world religion. The title "Fathers of the Church" refers to those who either had direct contact with the apostles or were sufficiently close to them to transmit their teaching with accuracy and fidelity. The early Fathers, specifically called Apostolic Fathers, include Saint Augustine and Saint Jerome, as well as many other less familiar names. Throughout history, great Christian thinkers and leaders would return again and again to the writings of these ancient Fathers as they tried to steer Christianity on a true course.

Returning to our story about the family for a moment, when we go through difficult times, moments of crisis or profound turning points in our life, we often look to our past, to our roots, for guidance. We return to the values we were brought up with, and we seek out those people that helped form us and make us what we are. And so, at this crucial point in the history of Christianity, as we near the second millenium, we also look to our roots, to our tradition, for guidance and direction.

6. Diverse Traditions

On our arrival back from our journey into the common tradition of old, one thing becomes rather apparent: throughout the centuries, we have developed a myriad of diverse traditions, all with their roots in the one common tradition. The reason why this has occurred is quite simple. The unchanging truths revealed to us by God must be applied to ever-changing cultural and historical situations. However, this application is quite complex. Christians have disagreed among themselves concerning precisely how the tradition should be applied and lived out in concrete historical circumstances. Thus, we do not find a uniform development stemming from the tradition, but rather a pluriform development. The roots remain the same, but there are diverging processes of development. To use an analogy from nature, Christianity is not like one long shoot springing from the ground, but instead is like a tree that has one solid base from which an intricate arrangement of branches grow. Throughout this book, we will be exploring the many historical circumstances within which varying traditions chose different routes to follow.

On hearing the word ecumenism, many people are under the mistaken impression that this means that the different routes taken by different traditions ought to merge into one common route. Nothing could be further from the essence of true ecumenism; unity does not imply uniformity. An example from our American immigrant experience illustrates this point very well.

Within our country we find some of the most ethnically mixed regions in the world. We have numerous instances of what is called ethnic pluralism. Within the confines of one city, we find a plurality of cultural groups living together. Even though they all share many things in common, they do not lose their identity and their uniqueness. We used to think of America as the "melting pot," but that turned out to be a rather misleading image since various cultural groups have affirmed the value of their heritages, retaining while transforming their identity.

Religious pluralism works in much the same way. There is no reason why we cannot be truly united as Christians and at the same time have a plurality of theologies, spiritualities, customs, laws, etc. There can be a real openness to one another rooted in our traditions while at the same time different groups remain loyal to the preservation of their own heritage (recall step two). Such an outlook is, in fact, inherent in Catholicism, which means "universal." There can be universal unity amid legitimate diversity; this is a seminal concept to which we shall return often.

Pluralism or pluriformity implies that one particular approach to God is not necessarily the only good approach or the only valuable approach. This is a hard concept for us as Catholics. In the past, we were quite convinced that we alone had the whole and absolute truth. But a shift in attitude must occur as we become aware that as a church, we are on pilgrimage, so to speak, and our formulation of the truth remains partial. Other traditions have valid contributions to make on our mutual journey toward God. Our God is a mystery, and as such, all of the church's formulations about God are not complete or absolute, but partial. We must pursue the truth together, listening to each other and in dialogue with each other, and allow room for legitimate diversity. The more we do this, the more catholic we allow our church to become:

> While preserving unity in essentials, let all members of the church, according to the office entrusted to each, preserve a proper freedom in the various forms of spiritual life and discipline, in the variety of liturgical rites, and even in the theological elaborations of revealed truth. In all things let charity be exercised. If the faithful are true to this course of action, they will be giving ever richer expression to the authentic catholicity of the church...(Decree on Ecumenism, art. 4).

7.   Set a Goal for the Future

What is our ultimate goal? It can be none other than that provided by Christ: "That they all be one." The aim of the ecumenical movement, as stated by the Faith and Order Commission of the World Council of Churches is:

> ...to proclaim the oneness of the Church of Jesus Christ and to call the churches to the goal of visible unity in one faith and one eucharistic fellowship, expressed in worship and common life in Christ, in order that the world might believe (By-Laws).

We have already stressed that such "visible unity" will not mean relinquishing our unique and cherished traditions. But if there will not be one, large, uniform "super-church," then what will there be? What is the shape of the unity to come?

Karl Rahner and Heinrich Fries, in *Unity and the Churches: An Actual Possibility*, hold out a vision of unity based on "fellowship," "reconciled diversity," and a model of "unity by stages." While this vision represents a concrete hope, there remains a degree of uncertainty because ecumenism is a process. We will only discover the stages as we move along.

It could be likened to a skillful glassblower who begins a piece of glass with certain materials and the rather vague goal of producing a beautiful piece of art. As the job begins, the glassblower sees the possibilities and is inspired in the process of working. The result is a beautiful and completely unique glass. Even though we can't see exactly what will emerge in the future, we can sketch out some possible models for Christian unity and will do so in later chapters.

We progress toward our goal as church on two distinct but related fronts. On the one hand, on an "official" level, we are engaged in the work toward unity. Professional theologians from the various traditions dialogue with each other. But on the other front, we must take our part, as the Vatican Council has requested. This book is provided to help you take your part. The two fronts need each other, and together we design the shape of our future unity. This is what step seven is all about—looking to the future and working toward it. In a sense, it underlies all of the previous steps. In each one you are doing your part. But in this step, there must be the distinct realization that you do not do this alone, completely by yourself, as you would engage in a personal hobby. It certainly involves study and private reflection, but finally it's something that the church, the people of God, engage in together.

The final word to be said regarding our method is perhaps the most important of all. As we work together, each step of the way, we must acknowledge that ecumenism is ultimately a gift from God. Ultimately unity is not something we accomplish by a particular method, but something God accomplishes through us. Our method is but one, small, limited way in which we can responsibly co-create with God the unity God desires. What God has in mind is always greater than what we can imagine. Aware of this we have the incentive to stretch our minds and expand our horizons.

SUMMARY

There is an inevitable abstractness to the method we have just discussed. As we move on now, we will be using the method, putting some flesh on the skeleton, so to speak. Each step of the way, one or another of the outlined steps will be at work, and occasionally explicit mention will again be made of one of the steps. To help you follow the method more easily, here is a summary of each step to refer to as you read and discuss what follows.

1.   A recognition of the separation that exists among Christians with an interest in removing this stumbling block.

2.   A two-fold conversion that includes both a) openness to those separated from us, and b) a deepened commitment to our own tradition.

3.   Reaching back in history to discover the origin of our separation by a) understanding the context within which the disagreements began, and b) recognizing that the context was often non-theological, reinforced by closed-minded attitudes.

4.   Returning to the present, a) recognizing that the disagreements and estrangements still exist; but b) without their original context, we're in a new situation in which there is no need for mutual alienation.

5.   Reaching back to our common tradition in Judaism, Jesus Christ, the Scriptures, and the Fathers.

6.   Returning to the present, realizing that while we share this common tradition, a) we have all built upon it in our unique traditions which b) contain a diversity that is good and helpful.

7.   We look to and work toward our future goal.

QUESTIONS
FOR REFLECTION AND DISCUSSION

1. What impels us to work toward Christian unity?

2. Why is the present disunity a scandal?

3. What are some of the ecumenical accomplishments already made? Discuss some of the attitudinal differences between now and 20 or 30 years ago.

4. What were your attitudes toward Protestant denominations as you grew up? Have you retained or rejected these attitudes?

5. What kind of experiences have you had ecumenically? Do you have close friends of a Protestant denomination? Do religious issues come up very often? Is there disagreement?

6. Can you describe the two key ideas that exist in "tension" with each other in regard to ecumenism (step two)? What does it mean to say that they exist in tension?

7. In light of this tension, do you foresee a time in which there will be real Christian unity? What do you think that unity will look like? Or does modern pluralism preclude reaching the ideal of unity?

8. Throughout history there has been a lack of balance between the two concepts of preserving and transforming. Which of the two have we tended to overemphasize?

9. Which side of the tension do you personally tend to gravitate towards more easily? Why? What experiences in your life as a Catholic have contributed to your own view?

10. What is the danger of focusing too exclusively on the concept of openness? Do you see areas in which this might be happening today?

11.   Why is it important to have a "sense of history" (step three). Can you think of an experience in your own life in which knowing the past background in a certain situation led you to a real insight about that situation?

12.   How would you characterize the attitude of young people toward their faith today? Are there advantages in trying to educate them ecumenically? How do you think they feel as they gradually come to realize the disunity that exists in Christianity?

13.   How might you incorporate an ecumenical spirit into your own dealings with young people (your own children or a religious education class)?

14.   What does it mean to say that America is a pluralistic nation? Why is the idea of pluralism so important for ecumenism?

15.   Do you have some experiences of ethnic pluralism, perhaps in your extended family? What are the kinds of attitudes necessary in order for various cultures to exist together in real harmony? Does this give us some clues about ecumenism?

CHAPTER TWO

A
History
of
Ecumenism

We are all aware of the bitter animosity that grew between Roman Catholics and other Christians during the centuries following Reformation. As one scholar has described it:

> Over much of Europe a mindset emerged that regarded Protestantism and Catholicism as mutually exclusive: one must be the true Christianity, the other a heretical Christianity. The vehemence with which fanatics on both sides viewed their religious enemies is suggested by a comment of Pope Paul IV: "Even if my own father were a heretic, I would gather the wood to burn him" (Minus, p.12).

While the intensity of religious conviction, alongside social and political pressures, caused the reformers to widen the gap, Roman Catholics became vigorously involved in attacking their new opponents and defending their own position—actions which came to be termed "the Counter Reformation."

Apologetics and Polemics   For nearly four centuries, the major forms of communication between Christian churches tended to be apologetics and polemics. Apologetics does not mean "apologizing" for one's position; rather, it means "defending one's position" against the arguments of a perceived opponent. There is a healthy type of apologetics. For example, when Christianity makes its case against atheism or secular humanism for the existence of a transcendent God who graciously reveals himself in human life, this would be called a Christian apologetic. But so urgent was the need during the Reformation for an apologetic among Christians that it deeply influenced the style and tone of Christian theologies until the twentieth century. Each side was involved—viciously at times—in the "my church is better than your church" syndrome. We all tend to fall into this attitude at times, with our churches, our houses and cars, and our accomplishments and successes. It is sinful tendency to assert our superiority over others, and no other such tendency is more of a hindrance to unity, whether among churches, families, or neighbors.

If apologetics means defending our own position, then, in order to assert the superiority of our arguments, we must "attack our opponent's position." This "attacking" is called polemics. Engaging in polemics is similar to engaging in apologetics, but polemics is directed toward the other party. For example, Catholics often described Martin Luther as one possessed by the devil, filled with falsehood, and prone to drunkenness and debauchery. Likewise, the pope was demeaned by other denominations and called the anti-Christ. We all tend to involve ourselves in polemics at times—all too often behind people's backs—and we know how destructive this activity can be. But such is the rut that Christian churches fell into throughout the post-Reformation centuries. Ecumenical conversion means getting out of such a rut, replacing defensive attitudes with trusting ones, showing a willingness to be renewed and transformed. Such a conversion of heart will profit our churches as well as our families, marriages, and friendships.

Ecumenical Pioneers   Prior to our own century, there were surprisingly few who had the courage to theologize ecumenically. There was a handful of dynamic people who tried hard to break through the walls that were being built, but their voices were drowned out in the polemics and apologetics of the times. Nonetheless, they began to develop innovative themes and ideas that in our own century would reach maturity and form positive foundations for more widespread ecumenical activity.

These ecumenical pioneers, journeying through a wilderness of indifference and bitterness, did not live to see the fruits of their labors. Not until the twentieth century was there a certain distance from which both sides could look back on the mutual scars inflicted by the Reformation and, having left behind formidable political, social, and psychological barriers, begin the slow and cautious task of healing. A brief outline will serve to highlight several of these voices. (See p. 26).

A Movement Begins   The first truly organized efforts toward ecumenism came from the Protestant Reformers. The impetus behind this effort is most interesting. Imagine yourself as a member of a primitive African tribe. One day some missionaries arrive and begin to tell you about a new religious outlook called Christianity. You find that what they have to say is very appealing. They move on but they leave behind the basic format of the new faith. Later, another group arrives, and you are delighted to find that they, too, are carrying the message of Christianity. However, you are dismayed at finding that these new missionaries label themselves differently from the previous group. They point out that their message has some variations in it in comparison to the previous one, and they make the needed corrections for you.

This in fact became a real problem for missionaries. There was too much diversity amid the one faith they were trying to share, which was proving to be a stumbling block, a scandal. This problem was the impetus behind a conference held in Edinburgh in 1910, a date that marks the beginning of the ecumenical movement. For the first time, different denominations were getting together to discuss some of their differences and mutual problems in the context of missions. In 1921, another step was taken when the International Missionary

1500

Pope Adrian VI pushes for reforms within Catholicism, but does not get far because of polemical attitudes toward Luther.

1517—onset of the Reformation

Desiderious Erasmus develops a program for religious peace based on mutual Christ-like love, and on the conviction that Catholics and Lutherans could disagree as long as there is a common adherence to certain essential doctrines.

George Cassander, like Erasmus, urges toleration of diversity in secondary matters.

1600

Christopher Davenport calls for a pact between Anglicans and Catholics, stressing the complementarity of the two positions.

Bishop Bossuet urges Protestants to re-examine Catholic doctrines and make accommodating gestures toward them.

1700

Luis du Pin initiates correspondence with the Anglican archbishop and they plan for a reunion that would stress common fundamentals and allow for diversity.

Justinius Febronius appeals for a restriction of papal power so as to facilitate reunion with German Protestants.

Johann Sailor encourages Christians to work together against the increasing impiety and infidelity caused by the age of Enlightment. The German Christian fellowship is formed.

1800

Johann Mohler evaluates Protestant positions with great respect and stresses nonjuridical aspects of Catholicism.

The Oxford movement in England recovers Catholic dimensions of Anglicanism. John Henry Newman coverts to Catholicism and makes a breach in Protestant prejudice (while warning Catholics not to try to *defeat* the Church of England, which would only be detrimental).

In 1857 the Association for the Promotion of the Unity of Christendom is established to foster prayer for Christian unity.

Council was formed. We can call these initial steps the first strand in the ecumenical movement.

Social and Ethical Concerns   A second strand began in 1925 with the first "Life and Work Conference" held in Stockholm. It was led by Nathan Soderblom, a Lutheran archbishop and scholar who was convinced that the Christian churches should become more involved with social and ethical concerns. A motto evolved out of this conference: "Doctrine divides, service unites." In this motto we find two distinct dimensions of any ecumenical effort. On the one hand there is doctrine, the systematized beliefs of various groups; on the other hand there is service, or the action that stems from one's belief. At first sight it seems easier to agree about service than it is to agree about doctrine. Two denominations may have two entirely different doctrines on the meaning of the eucharist, but they might well agree—without hesitation—to help starving people. However, when service involves politics, severe tensions can easily arise between groups, as has been the case recently.

Thus, the viewpoint of the Life and Work Conference was primarily practical; it concerned itself with working together on various projects that required no preliminary doctrinal agreement. World War I had ended and there were endless social problems in its wake: Should the *laissez-faire* policy of capitalism be condemned? What stand should be taken on social rights? What position ought to be taken on Bolshevism? These were the types of issues discussed by the Conference.

Questions of Doctrine   Although these questions are practical ones, there is a theoretical side or a doctrinal side to them as well. For example, how do you talk about church/state relations without asking the more theoretical question about the nature of the church? "Doctrine divides, service unites" has a certain truth to it, but it is also simplistic. Because of the need to also discuss issues on a doctrinal level, a third strand of the ecumenical movement was born: the Faith and Order Conferences. These began in 1927 in Lausanne, Switzerland. A second one took place in Edinburgh in 1937.

These three different strands of the ecumenical movement were gradually incorporated in 1948 into one larger and more cohesive unit, the "World Council of Churches." It remains active today, and has convened six times since its birth.

Roman Catholic Response   The Roman Catholic involvement in these new ecumenical beginnings is quite complex. Though officially, Catholicism was cautious, there were many transforming forces within the church that heralded a new era of Catholic ecumenism. In retrospect, both official and unofficial forces helped strike a healthy balance as Catholicism edged closer toward the mature position that emerged at Vatican II.

When the Christian traditions were preparing for the Life and Work, and Faith and Order Conferences in the 1920 s, they also invited Catholics to be represented at these meetings. At each invitation, however, there was a refusal from the papacy. The presupposition behind this refusal was the conviction that Catholicism already had the inherent unity that was the goal of these other various efforts. The only way for other Christians to engage themselves in true unity would be for them to convert to Catholicism. Such an approach certainly has an apologetic character, but for important reasons.

At issue was a struggle between different "models" of the mutual goal of reunion. The first model insists that reunion is equivalent to conversion on the part of all individual Christian churches, while the second (and more nebulous) model offers the possibility of "corporate reunion" in which churches would retain their own identities under an official, common, catholic bond. Catholicism would cautiously move toward the latter model, but not without bringing to it the best of the former: that real conversion is needed if reunion is to be authentic. But Catholics would also reevaluate this demand for conversion, no longer defining it so narrowly as to make a demand only on the Reformers but instead also seeing the need for renewal among themselves.

As we said earlier, the initial Catholic response to the new ecumenical movement was to refuse to join the others at the Faith and Order Conferences. In 1928, Pope Pius XI took a more drastic step. He wrote the encyclical *Mortalium animos* in which he condemned the ecumenical movement. In addition to forbidding Catholic participation in the movement, he accused it of being founded on error and illusion and, hence, said it was bound to fail. Pius felt that the movement was trying to reach unity by too easy a compromise, by trying to find the "least common denominator" in creedal statements and by focusing too exclusively on service.

While this action was definitely negative since it discouraged many ecumenical pioneers, there was also something positive about it. Pius had sounded a note of caution, and as we saw in the first chapter, caution is most crucial in developing an ecumenical theology. A pastoral letter written in response to the Decree on Ecumenism captures well the original foresight of Pius' move:

> Two generations ago, when the ecumenical movement began in the Protestant and Anglican Churches, there were many voices suggesting that the question of truth did not matter. The slogan used in those days was that doctrine divides while service unites. Since that time, partially due to the entry of the Eastern Orthodox Churches into our ecumenical movement, these voices have become rare among our separated brethren. Today, Protestant, Anglican, and Lutheran Christians realize that such a pragmatic approach to Christian unity ultimately results in confusion (Abbott, Documents, quoted on p. 339).

The next pontiff, Pius XII, sounded a more optimistic note. In 1939 his first encyclical *Summi pontificatus* offered unprecedented friendliness and acknowledged the good will of the Protestants. In this sentence from the encyclical, notice the shift from apologetic theology toward an ecumenical theology:

> We cannot pass over in silence the profound impression of heartfelt gratitude made on us by the good wishes of those who, though not belonging to the visible body of the Catholic Church, have given noble and sincere expression to their expression of all that unites them to us, in love for the person of Christ or in belief in God.

While Pius XII was more positive about the ecumenical movement, he was still cautious. For example, he issued a letter in which he allowed Catholics to take part in dialogue with Protestants, but the sole purpose of such interaction would be to invite those separated back to the one, true fold. The move for a model of reunion that was not as condescending remained on the horizon.

Changes Affecting Catholic Ecumenism   While the magisterium was sounding needed notes of caution, bold strokes of ecumenical initiative were being made on other Catholic fronts. Let us consider several events which heralded the ecumenical climate we inherit today.

A changed atmosphere in the twentieth century lent to improved inter-church relations. This was the age of communication. We had become a global village in which people and nations had to dialogue in order to survive and grow. Pressed ever closer by new technological breakthroughs and increasing interdependence, an attitude of tolerance and mutual cooperation was of the essence.

Amid such positive advancements, our century also brought with it the tragedy of two world wars. These threats to cherished institutions and values were a new stimulus for solidarity among churches. A striking example of this solidarity occurred in 1943. An American ship was sinking, and some of the men did not have life preservers. Four chaplains—a Catholic, a Jew, and two Protestants—gave their life preservers to four of the men. They met their deaths on the sinking ship with arms locked in prayer.

A more commonplace example was the simple sharing of church buildings. The great ecumenist Yves Congar was greatly influenced by a childhood experience of church sharing. After the Catholic church had been burned by German soldiers, a warm-hearted Protestant congregation readily shared their place of worship.

In 1879, Pope Leo XIII in *Aeterni patris"* had urged a rediscovery of the writings of St. Thomas Aquinas among Catholic scholars. While giving Catholic scholarship and seminary training a new cohesiveness, this revival also led to increased respect for the positions of outsiders. According to Thomistic philosophy, every event in history has meaning and purpose and is providentially guided. Errors abound, but every error not only contains some truth but also, by way of contrast and conflict, furthers our discovery of the truth. Thus, nothing is to be discarded as useless. Thus, theologians such as Josef Lortz and Yves Congar began to reevaluate and reinterpret Luther and the Reformation. Congar, called by some "the father of Catholic ecumenism," developed many of the themes that would eventually surface officially—to his delight—in the Decree on Ecumenism.

Other Christian traditions were undergoing currents of change in which they recovered themes that were intrinsically Catholic. Some of these churches had undergone a rather thorough liberalizing of theological attitudes. Humanity and its innate capacities—following patterns set by the Age of Enlightenment—had been glorified, while the transcendence of God had been minimized. But now, especially through the genius of Karl Barth, a phase of neo-Orthodoxy recovered themes strongly in tune with Roman Catholicism. In addition to an emphasis on the transcendence of God, a new liturgical movement was underway. It was recovering early Christian roots shared by Catholics—who were themselves experiencing liturgical renewal. Ranking high among such recoveries was a renewed sense of the centrality of the eucharist in Christian life.

Perhaps the most crucial ecumenical change that occurred was that separated Christians began to pray for one another and for reunion. In the 1930s, Fr. Paul Couturier introduced the Octave of Prayer for Christian Unity during which all those participating would pray for forgiveness and for restoration of unity. We still mark this week of prayer each January.

Finally, the "return to Rome" model of reunion was virtually abandoned. The ecumenical pioneers had uncovered the basic fault of such a model: All Christians, in their experience, had their own unique treasures regarding the Christian faith. Even Pope Pius XI acknowledged this. In the 1920s, referring to the Eastern Churches, he said "The separated particles of gold-bearing rock themselves contain gold." The "return to Rome" model had risked losing such treasures, which, in their diversity, enliven and enrich the faith. This realization was the primary impetus behind carving out a new model for re-union, a difficult and delicate task we are still working at today.

The Second Vatican Council   Against the backdrop of the biblical, liturgical, and ecumenical movements that were already underway in Catholicism, Pope Pius XII's successor, Pope John XXIII, opened a new era in the church with his warm and friendly personality and his convocation of the Second Vatican Council. When he convoked the council, he told the world it would be:

> ...a demonstration of the church, always living and always young, which feels the rhythm of the times and which in every century beautifies herself with new splendor, radiates new light, achieves new conquests, while remaining identical in herself, faithful to the divine image impressed on her countenance... (quoted in Abbott, Documents, p.706).

An important distinction can be drawn from this quotation. On one hand, Pope John speaks of the unchanging deposit of faith handed on through the ages. On the other, he points out that the way faith is formulated or expressed needs to be adapted or changed to fit the times. John clarified this theme with these words:

> The deposit of faith is one thing; the way that it is presented is another. For the truth preserved in our sacred doctrine can retain the same substance and meaning under different forms of expression (Abbott, p. 349).

One reason there can be a developing variety of formula-tions of our faith is that God, the object of our faith, is a mystery. A mystery has a certain fullness that we can never completely, once and for all, capture and formulate. We can and must try to articulate God's revelation to us, but ultimately our formulations will fall short of the fullness of this great and absolute mystery.

Secretariat for Christian Unity   One of the definitive actions of John XXIII was to form the Secretariat for the Pro-motion of Christian Unity. For the first time there was an official body within the Catholic Church that was ecumenically oriented. It was organized in 1961 by the late Augustin Cardinal Bea, a biblical scholar. In the United States, this ecumenical orientation is continued through the Bishop's Committee on Ecumenical and Interreligious Affairs, and on the local level, through diocesan Ecumenical and Interfaith offices. Thus, from an official and organizational viewpoint we can see the radical shift away from an attitude of preservation toward real transformation leading to unity. Of course, such official manifestations of ecumenism must work in concert with an ecumenical spirit implanted in the hearts of all the faithful in order for genuine unity to take place. When John XXIII died in 1963, before the completion of the Council, Paul VI continued the bold program of renewal.

Decree on Ecumenism   In 1964, the Council's Decree on Ecumenism, with a fully developed ecumenical theology, was issued. The initial draft of the Decree was not well received because of its cautionary attitude. When the Council fathers voted that a new document be forged, the chief responsibility was handed to Cardinal Bea and the Secretariat. The new document, favorably received, moved away from the "return to Rome" model of reunion by advocating renewal on all fronts toward the goal of "full ecclesiastical reunion." For reunion to take place, the document stated, there must be willingness to learn from one another, to become mutually enriched by each other's treasures, and to grow together.

Scripture Sharing   A striking example of learning from one another is in the area of sacred Scripture. Traditionally, Catholic theology has spoken of two sources of revelation from God, Scripture and tradition. But Catholics have tended to overemphasize the latter, while other Christian traditions have given priority to the former. With a new interest in Scripture, generated by the Second Vatican Council, both sides are now more open to reconciling and balancing Scripture and tradition.

For Catholics, this has had several positive effects. Chief among them is that the language of the Vatican II documents is strikingly biblical. As opposed to the more cautionary language that had appeared previously, the warmth, openness, and familiarity of biblical language gives the documents a wide, non-threatening appeal. Also in our liturgies, the word of God has been given increased respect and emphasis. Biblical discussion and study groups have naturally flowed from this emphasis.

We should say here that in the area of biblical scholarship, Catholics stand on the shoulders of their forerunners from other Christian churches. These scholars have paved the way by discovering and developing critical tools to fully investigate the biblical texts. Mutual enrichment on all sides has been offered to Catholics through the spirit of dialogue and consensus, which springs directly from the Second Vatican Council.

Vatican II to the Present   Ecumenical activity has taken place on many levels since the Council. There has been shared prayer and worship, shared Bible study groups, joint cooperation and collaboration on scholarly issues, common use of buildings and facilities, cooperation in social issues, meetings between church leaders and joint ecumenical working and dialogue groups.

The dialogues that have taken place are quite impressive and the list of them runs long. In the chapters to come, we will get a glimpse of some of the most successful of these dialogues. If you wish to explore one or more of them in greater depth, then, of course, you will want to read the dialogue results listed in the bibliography as well as the following chapters. To learn more about the dialogues, let us explore several aspects.

Nature of Dialogue   A dialogue group normally consists of church leaders and professional theologians who gather at regular intervals to discuss crucial issues that both divide and unite the communions involved. The discussions, and published results, illuminate areas of convergence and divergence. The "Agreed Statements" that often result are not yet officially sanctioned by church leadership on either side, even though the leadership encourages the dialogues to take place. Official sanction is a step that is further along on the agenda of reunion.

There are four major topics that appear over and over again in many of the dialogues.

1. BAPTISM   This is a perfect starting point for dialogue and a promising area of convergence.

2. EUCHARIST   The whole concept and reality of sacrament, so central to the Christian tradition, involves baptism and eucharist since those are the two key sacraments shared by all Christians.

3. MINISTRY   Every Christian community has developed traditions to insure that the mission of Jesus and the proclamation of the good news is continued.

4. AUTHORITY   This topic is crucial in all ecumenical dialogues and is essentially the question of the necessity and validity of the Roman Catholic papacy. The papacy is the one distinctive feature of the Catholic tradition that sharply contrasts with the leadership styles of other traditions, and it appears to be a primary barrier to reunion. But, on the other hand, one thesis of this book is that the papacy might, in fact, turn out to be the primary forces for achieving future unity. Its role will be essential toward fulfilling Jesus' desire "that all may be one."

In addition to these four primary topics, many other topics are discussed in these dialogues, for example, the creed or creeds, spirituality, inter-marriage, intercommunion, and moral decision-making.

As we have already mentioned, the dialogue results are published in the form of agreed statements and summaries of the discussion and preparatory papers. These documents allow us to discover areas of agreement as well as areas that remain to be resolved. A note of caution should be issued in regard to their style. Concerning the agreed statements, for example, it is best to quote from the foreword of one of the documents:

> It must be remembered that the statements are consensus statements: each word in them was agreed to by all members of the Consultation. That means that the statements are not verbose; extra words will not be found in them. Sentences could sometimes be paragraphs, paragraphs a chapter, and a chapter a book (ARCIC Final Report, p. iv).

Thus, should you venture into these statements, which we highly recommend, do not expect to find lively reading. Other sections of the published results presuppose a certain theological background and these also make for heavy reading. (I'm hoping that this book will sufficiently capture the spirit of the dialogues so that educated Catholics who are not theologians will have a sense of their progress.)

The dialogues between individual churches led, in 1982, to the "Common Christian Statement." In that year, the Faith and Order Commission of the World Council of Churches, with Roman Catholic participation, developed a document on common Christian beliefs about baptism, eucharist, and ministry. This document, referred to as the Lima Statement, is "must" reading. The Lima Statement is the first realization of the theological basis for fellowship. The next step will be the Commission's study, "Toward the Common Expression of the Apostolic Faith Today."

The most important accomplishment of dialoguing has been the realization that ecumenical discussion should not remain only on an "upper-echelon" level. As one of the architects of the Anglican/Roman Catholic dialogue points out:

> There would in fact be a danger of ecumenical dialogue being restricted to discussions among theologians and specialists without the individual member of the faithful, of average Christian education, ever coming to grips with what is at stake in these discussions and understanding the implications of the desired consensus. What would be the value of a church union born merely of the toil and love of a little group of experts? (ARC-DOC II, p.5).

Thus, the ultimate ecumenical challenge is to each of us. The dialogues point beyond themselves to the real source of sound ecumenism—our own conversions.

An Ecumenical Attitude   In Pope John Paul II's first encyclical letter, *Redemptor hominis*, he strikes a fine balance between the desire for unity and fidelity to our own faith tradition. The following quote summarizes well the recent history of ecumenism and the ecumenical attitude that must take root in all of us.

What shall I say of all the initiatives that have sprung from the new ecumenical orientation? The unforgettable Pope John XXIII set out the problem of Christian unity with evangelical clarity as a simple consequence of the will of Jesus Christ himself, our Master, the will that Jesus stated on several occasions but to which he gave expression in a special way in his prayer in the upper room the night before he died: "I pray...Father...that they may all be one." The Second Vatican Council responded concisely to this requirement with its decree on ecumenism. Pope Paul VI, availing himself of the activities of the Secretariat for prompting Christian Unity, began the first difficult steps on the road to the attainment of that unity. Have we gone far along that road? ...we can say that we have made real and important advances. And one thing is certain; we have worked with perseverance and consistency, and the representatives of other Christian Churches and Communities have also committed themselves together with us, for which we are heartily grateful to them....We must therefore seek unity without being discouraged at the difficulties that can appear or accumulate along that road; otherwise, we would be unfaithful to the word of Christ, we would fail to accomplish his testament. Have we the right to run this risk?

There are people who in the face of difficulties or because they consider that the first ecumenical endeavors have brought negative results that would have liked to turn back. Some even express the opinion that these efforts are harmful to the cause of the gospel, are leading to a further rupture in the church, are causing confusion of ideas in questions of faith and morals and are ending up with a specific indifferentism. It is perhaps a good thing that the spokesman for these opinions should express their fears. However, in this respect also, correct limits must be maintained. It is obvious that this new stage in the church's life demands of us a faith that is particularly aware, profound, and responsible. True ecumenical activity means openness, drawing closer, availability for dialogue, and a shared investigation of the truth in the full evangelical and Christian sense. But in no way does it or can it mean giving up or in any way diminishing the treasures of divine truth that the church has constantly confessed and taught. To all who, for whatever motive, would wish to dissuade the church from seeking the universal unity of Christians the question must once again be put: Have we the right not to do it? Can we fail to have trust—in

spite of all human weakness and all the faults of past centuries—
in our Lord's grace as revealed recently through what the Holy
Spirit said and we heard during the council?

QUESTIONS
FOR REFLECTION AND DISCUSSION

1.   Do you think that Christian churches today exhibit a
defensive attitude? In which ways?

2.   What historical events may have influenced the churches
to question how they related to one another?

3.   Should the churches lay some of their traditions aside for
the sake of unity?

4.   How do you react to the efforts of our ecumenical
pioneers?

5.   From your experience, who are people that you consider
to be ecumenical pioneers? Why?

6.   What is your reaction to the statement "Doctrine divides,
service unites"?

7.   Can there be unity without doctrinal agreement?

8.   In the areas of doctrine, community, and service, what
do you see as unifying or dividing factors between Catholicism
and other Christian traditions?

9.   How would you describe your present attitude toward
other Christian traditions?

10.   What can you do to promote unity among Christians?

11.   Does Pope John Paul's encyclical statement reflect any
official change in the Roman Catholic position toward
ecumenism?

12.   How close are we to realizing the dream of unity?

CHAPTER THREE

Early
Christianity

Jesus Christ spent his public life traveling through the Holy Land telling about the kingdom of God, emphasizing that the kingdom had begun. He gave his followers a command and mission to go make disciples of all nations, and when his work was accomplished, the outpouring of the Holy Spirit took place on Pentecost. This event is often called "the birthday of the church." The Holy Spirit would forever guide and sanctify the followers of Jesus. The history of the church had begun; the first community at Jerusalem was formed.

The apostles soon left Jerusalem to preach the gospel to other communities. Zeal to "convert all nations" and early persecutions further scattered the early disciples. In an astonishingly short time, small Christian communities had sprung up in all main centers of the Roman empire and even in places beyond the Roman frontiers.

In the early days of Christianity, the basic unit was the community in each city—the local church headed by the bishop who was aided in administration by the presbyters (or elders) and deacons. The local church, in union with other local churches, formed the communion of churches: the universal church. The smaller communities in the surrounding countryside depended on the church of the city, which was recognized as the "mother church" of the area. The role of the eucharist in manifesting and realizing the unity of the local church was already taken for granted by Ignatius of Antioch at the beginning of the second century. In his view, the church is the eucharistic community, which fully realizes its true nature when it celebrates the Lord's Supper. In the second century this celebration took place in each community with the bishop normally presiding.

By the end of the second century, certain local churches were recognized as exercising the leadership over the other local churches of an area. The churches so recognized were usually ones that were associated with one or more of the apostles. The bishops of these principal sees (centers of authority) were preeminent over their fellow bishops, especially in the matter of the consecration of new bishops for the local churches of their area.

With the edict of Milan (issued by the Roman Emperor Constantine in 313), the church became closely connected to the vast Roman empire. As the empire continued to expand, it was divided into manageable administrative units. The broadest division was simply between East and West. Christians had to work out their own administrative system, and they basically did this along the same lines as the empire. Thus, there came to be a basic division between "Eastern Rite" Christians and "Western Rite" Christians. The word "rite" referred to not only liturgical practices, but also their entire ecclesiastical discipline and spiritual heritage.

There were also other divisions in the church in addition to the initial one between East and West. There were five major administrative centers and these were known as patriarchates. It is easiest to think of this division as a hub with five spokes. In the center is Jerusalem. To the West of the hub is Rome. To the South is Alexandria. The City of Antioch lies to the North, but it controlled the region that lay to the East of Jerusalem. Finally, to the North lay Constantinople.

Rome was recognized as enjoying a certain primacy as the guardian of orthodoxy. The pope, bishop of Rome and patriarch of the West, was considered to be the first bishop in the church.

One of the key cultural differences among the patriarchates was language. In the East, Greek was the principal
language. In the West, Latin predominated. As you may know
from experience, if you travel in a foreign country, but don't
know the language, you truly feel "foreign." If you travel to
an English-speaking country like England or Ireland, you feel
more at home because at least you can understand what people
are saying, even if they have other cultural traits that differ
from your own. Thus, language can be a formidable barrier
and can easily separate people.

Another area of differences was worship. In the early
church there was a great variety and freedom in liturgical
worship. The bishops, preserving the substance of Christ's
mandate, felt free to improvise the prayers of the Divine Services, including the Eucharistic Liturgy, yet all used a generally
accepted outline. By the fourth century, liturgical prayers
became standardized.

Eventually the influence exercised by the metropolitan
churches was extended to the liturgy as well. Daughter churches
patterned their liturgical services on those of the mother
churches and sometimes adopted their customs completely.
From three major liturgical families (Antioch, Alexandria,
Rome) others emerged, developing and growing according to
the customs of the peoples involved. These "families" as well
as other liturgical sub-divisions are sometimes called rites. (See
the accompanying chart for a listing of the major liturgical
families.)

During the fourth and fifth centuries, the principal sees
developed a working relationship (called taxis) for handling
disputes in church matters. At Nicaea in 325, the First Ecumenical Council sketched out this relationship in regard to
Rome, Alexandria, and Antioch (while granting an honorary
precedence to Jerusalem after Antioch). With the Council of
Chalcedon in 451, this arrangement also included Constantinople.

When problems arose in the early church, the bishops
gathered together and tried to work them out. If the problem
was a minor one, restricted to a small portion of the empire,
only the bishops from that region would gather. However, if

GENEALOGY OF THE CHRISTIAN
CHURCHES/NATIONALITIES/LITURGIES

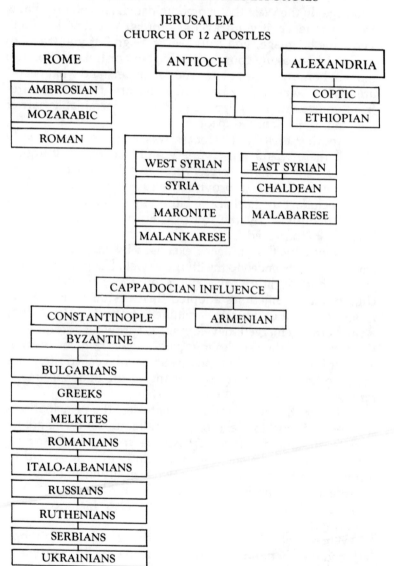

(Genealogy from *The Eastern Churches: Los Angeles Pastoral* Directory, Los Angeles: Archdiocese of Los Angeles, 1978. Used with permission.)

there were a problem that involved the entire church, then a larger council would be held. These larger councils came to be known as ecumenical councils from the Greek word, *oikoumene*, meaning "the entire inhabited world." Within the setting of these ecumenical councils, early stages of breakdown in relations were evident—a breakdown that eventually led to the radical separation of East and West.

Early Church Problems   The councils held during the early centuries of Christianity dealt with a variety of problems, but foremost among them was the hotly debated question of who Jesus Christ really was. Theologians term this the problem of Christology. Since the very center of our faith is Jesus Christ, this has been a perennial concern throughout the centuries. We must carefully consider this problem, in the setting of the ecumenical councils, since it was the main source of division in the early church.

The original apostles experienced Jesus as a real man, like themselves. At first they probably did not know him as the Son of God in any unique way, though they certainly knew there was something special about him. After Jesus' death and resurrection, they began to reconsider the events they had experienced with him. In light of his resurrection, they came to the gradual conclusion that he was not only human, but also divine.

It doesn't make sense, from a purely rational viewpoint, that one person could be both God and man at the same time. It is a paradox. And since it is not an easy thing to explain, it is obvious that people will make mistakes when they try to talk about it. Basically, early Christians made two types of mistakes—mistakes we continue to make today. On the one hand, they made the mistake of letting the divinity of Jesus completely overshadow his humanness. The extreme tendency here was to think of him as a God who simply appeared to be human but really wasn't, at least not completely. You may recall thinking, perhaps in your childhood, that Jesus didn't really suffer when he was crucified, since he was God and God can't feel pain. This position, defined as heretical in the early church, is called Docetism (from the Greek *dokeo*, "to seem").

Although the heresy itself soon vanished, the concept behind it would continue to trouble the church through the centuries. It is the impulse to see material, bodily creation as somehow inferior and distasteful. A broader movement known as Gnosticism in the early church had favored such a "dualism" between matter and spirit, and thus lay the groundwork for groups like the Docetists. They considered it unimaginable that God could assume a grossly inferior human body.

On the other hand, some early Christians made the mistake of over-emphasizing the humanity of Jesus. If Jesus were really divine, then how could he have entered into our human condition, totally and completely? How can we relate with someone who is divine and doesn't share in the perplexities of our human experience? It was concluded that Jesus must be a true and complete man, and "divinity" would consist only in his being such an extraordinary and exemplary man. This view was held by a priest from Alexandria named Arius and was thus termed "Arianism." It, too, was defined as heretical by the early church.

This synopsis is only a simplification of the intricate Christological debates, but it gives us a feel for the difficulty of coming to a conclusion about who Jesus really is. One of the problems is that in defining him, we are making a formulation about him. Formulations always fall short of the reality they are trying to express. Jesus Christ, God and man, is a mysterious paradox, and a paradox cannot be easily explained or defined. Or, to put it differently, Jesus Christ is the self-revelation of God, and God (an absolute mystery) cannot be easily explained or defined.

Response of the Early Councils   The Patriarch of Constaninople, Nestorius, held opinions about the nature of Jesus Christ that were suspect, especially among respected monks. Nestorius was determined to do justice to both the divinity and humanity of Jesus Christ, the acknowledged savior of all. Thus, he tended to separate the two "natures" of Jesus rather than think of them together. In the process, he over-emphasized the humanity of Jesus. Nestorius began by asserting that Mary could not rightfully be called *Theotokos*, translated as the mother or bearer of God, but rather should be called the mother of the man Jesus. He went on to demonstrate that in Jesus there were two persons, co-joined, but remaining separate persons nonetheless. The man Jesus was like a temple in which God dwelt. It was not God and man that suffered and died, but only the "man."

Nestorius had a bitter opponent from Alexandria named Cyril. As Cyril saw it, Nestorius' teaching allowed only an extrinsic relationship between the divine and human dimensions of Christ. This made the Incarnation an illusion, and redemption was meaningless since only an ordinary man had died for us. Cyril countered this by stressing the unity of the divine and human natures in Christ. Yet for Cyril, the full humanity of Jesus was hard to swallow. He had difficulty with the scriptural passages describing Jesus as sad or weak and, what was even more crucial, dying. His tendency was to overemphasize the divinity of Jesus and downplay his humanity.

In 431, at the Council of Ephesus (the third Ecumenical Council), the teaching of Nestorius was condemned. There were not two persons in Christ, but rather one person who had two natures, human and divine.

Generally accepted doctrine, which was clarified at Ephesus, was called Orthodox. Those who rejected this doctrine were called heretics. At the council of Ephesus there were many who disagreed with the Christological formula that had resulted. Those who disagreed were from the patriarchates of Jerusalem and Antioch (which was Nestorius' original home). Those who resided in Alexandria, Rome, and Constaninople were considered Orthodox. Thus, there were some Eastern Rite Christians, those from Jerusalem and Antioch, who were no longer Orthodox. They created the Assyrian Church of the East, which is present in the United States today as well as in Iran and Iraq. In India it is known as the Malabar Church.

The Council of Chalcedon   Now let us consider another ecumenical council that revealed even more divisions in Christianity. This one was held at Chalcedon in 451, and again the topic was Christology. At the Council of Ephesus the conclusion was reached that Jesus Christ was one person with two natures. Afterward, in Egypt (Cyril's territory), a doctrine we call monophysitism began to develop. In English this might be translated as "one-nature-ism." As you might deduce, this teaching was that after the Incarnation, Jesus Christ was not only one person, but also one nature—the human was absorbed into the divine. At Chalcedon, this was condemned, and this Orthodox doctrine was proclaimed: Christ is one person consisting of two natures, divine and human. This famous doctrine has come to be known as the Chalcedonian formula. For centuries it has served to hold together the paradoxical union of the divine and human in Jesus Christ and to clarify the mystery of the Incarnation.

As at Ephesus, not all agreed with the Chalcedonian formula. This time, those from Alexandria, Egypt, where the condemned doctrine originated, rejected the teaching of the council and so were no longer considered Orthodox. By this time, only those Christians from the patriarchates of Rome and Constantinople were considered Orthodox. Those who did not totally accept the decisions of this council were known as Monophysite Christians (believers in one nature). They are more properly called the non-Chalcedonians. This division claimed the Coptic Church in Egypt, the Ethiopian Church, the Western Syrian or Jacobite Church, the Syrian Church of India, and the Armenian Church. The churches involved in these fifth-century divisions are often called by other names: the Lesser Eastern Churches, the Oriental Orthodox, or the Ancient Eastern Churches.

In recent years there has been much discussion about the actual doctrinal differences of these churches. There have been fruitful ecumenical exchanges between them and the Roman Church. The most significant took place in May of 1980 when Pope John Paul II and the late Ignatius Yacoub II, Syrian Orthodox patriarch of Antioch and of the whole East, met in Rome. Both pledged their desire and effort to become united in one faith and common practice. It is recognized that both the Roman Catholic Church and these Oriental churches hold very similar positions on Christology. They continue to work on a common formula that would reestablish full communion.

QUESTIONS
FOR REFLECTION AND DISCUSSION

1. In what ways is the church today like the early church?

2. Are there differences between the church today and the early church that have ecumenical significance?

3. Do you know of any contemporary groups who over-emphasize the humanity (or divinity) of Jesus?

4. How has your view of Jesus changed over the years?

5. To what extent do you feel that personal and cultural differences affect our view of Jesus?

6. Are there any alternatives to condemning a heresy?

CHAPTER FOUR

The Orthodox Tradition

Historians generally recognize that the event called the Great Schism cannot be exactly dated. This schism involved the two larger portions of the church at that time: The Roman Church and the Byzantine Church. By the tenth century the Byzantine Church (also called the Church of Constantinople) extended from Greece to countries such as Bulgaria, Serbia, Romania, and Russia. Its influence was well established in the Eastern patriarchates of Antioch, Alexandria, and Jerusalem, as well as in the Slavic countries, while the Roman Church had spread throughout the Western world.

The division between these groups came about gradually as a result of a long complicated process, starting well before the eleventh century and not completed until some time after it. Many different influences were at work. The division was conditioned by cultural, political, and economic factors; it then developed into a theological quarrel. Long before there was an open division between East and West, the two sides were becoming strangers. The Christian East involved in this rift came to be known as the Orthodox or Eastern Orthodox Church. The West was called the Catholic Church.

The Great Schism   One of the first things to remember is that no one particular event sparked the eventual separation. It was a gradual process, and much of the estrangement was due to cultural differences.

Between the reigns of Leo and Charlemagne—fifth to the eighth century—the western part of the Roman Empire disintegrated under pressure from "barbarian" mass invasions. Large sections of the Eastern half succumbed to the political and religious force of Islam. The Christian civilization was decaying in both East and West and with decay came increased isolation.

During the ninth, tenth and eleventh centuries, this lack of contact between the two parts of the church accentuated the differences in their respective religious practices. Eventually the two groups became intolerant of each other. They disagreed over liturgical innovations and whether clergy should marry (which the East has always allowed). The primary difficulty was that neither side was willing to conduct the kind of delicate negotiations that were needed to remain cohesive.

Because of this inability to communicate, a disastrous event took place in 1054. Due to some political differences, as well as differences concerning religious practices, a papal delegation excommunicated the leaders of the Eastern Church, who in turn excommunicated the papal delegation. These two mutual anathemas did not in and of themselves cause the schism, but they did provide the ammunition that fueled the eventual separation.

In 1204, crusaders from the West, breaking out of the centuries-old isolation, set out to capture Jerusalem back from the Moslems. They ended up conquering Constantinople instead. They installed a Western patriarch there, and forced the reigning Eastern patriarch to leave the city. Imagine the bitterness that resulted from such an act! This event naturally undermined further efforts at reunion. As one commentator put it, "The barbarous behavior of the Western crusaders...followed by the sixty-year-old Latin empire in the East, made hatred of the West something that Easterners imbibed with their mother's milk" (Piepkorn I:33).

Attempts at Reunion   The two principal attempts to reunite the churches took place at the Second Council of Lyons in 1274, and at the Council of Florence in 1439. Documents were signed at the latter Council, and these showed genuine interest in reunion. The primary reason both attempts failed was a lack of understanding and cooperation among the people involved. For example, because advance groundwork had not been done, the Greek signatories were treated as traitors when they went back home.

In 1453, the Turks conquered Constantinople and put pressure on the patriarch there to formally renounce the reunion documents. From that time on, all relations between East and West were severed.

The real tragedy of the schism is that political concerns and cultural differences played too large a role. Throughout the second millennium, the two churches developed independently, and today there are some real barriers that must be overcome from a doctrinal viewpoint. Though ecumenical discussion must focus on doctrines, the underlying problem remains the differences in culture. There are really two different, though distantly related, civilizations involved.

As Roman Catholics and Orthodox Catholics enter into dialogue, there are many key issues that will come to the fore. Here we will discuss three of them: knowledge of God, the Trinity, and ecumenical councils.

1.   Knowledge of God

Try to imagine the different ways in which people communicate with God. There are as many approaches as there are people! As we said in Chapter One, there exists a real pluralism of approaches to God. Some people find that they relate best to God with the help of external stimuli. For example: a silent church filled with beautiful statues and stained glass; Rosary beads or prayer booklets; a silent time with nature where the presence of God in the majesty of creation can be felt. Another approach involves "letting go" of created things to enter into wordless contemplation of the mystery of God.

There are many approaches to spirituality, but there exist two basic modes of approaching God. In the first, we allow created things and persons to mediate (be a "go-between") in our relationship to God. This is called *kataphatic* knowledge of God (the word comes from the Greek, meaning assertion or statement). It emphasizes the immanence of God, that is, God's closeness and availability to us in creation. The second approach, (with no "go-between") is called the *apophatic* way. It emphasizes the transcendence of God, God's otherness, or the fact that God is completely beyond our world. The *apophatic* approach to God creates the awareness that any type of formulation is ultimately inadequate in the face of God, the absolute mystery. When formulation is necessary, it speaks of what God is not.

Both these approaches are valid and helpful. In the Bible, we encounter a God who is both involved in our world and our history and still infinitely beyond it, both immanent and transcendent. A good place to find both of these aspects is in the psalms, the "prayer-book" of the Israelites, which the Christian tradition has inherited and widely used. For example, read Psalm 23 and then Psalm 33. You can experience in these psalms pluralism of approaches to God. To connect for a moment to our discussion of Christology, look in the New Testament for signs of both the human and divine natures of Jesus, which correspond respectively to God's immanence and transcendence. In both the East and the West, spiritual writers have described both the *kataphatic* and the *apophatic* modes.

There is a slight technical difference in the theories the two sides have concerning knowledge of God. The theology involved is complex, and here we will present only the most basic differences. In Western tradition, both the *kataphatic* and *apophatic* approaches offer us imperfect knowledge of God. We never see God in a comprehensive way. We might learn something new about God each day of our lives, even into eternity, and we would still not know God completely.

In the Eastern tradition, it is also held that we can never know God completely. However, in the East, the *apophatic* mode is considered to give a person a superior knowledge of God. It is based on an understanding of real participation in the divine life by grace and faith, *theosis*. The aim of the Christian life is a personal confrontation with the living God in Trinity. At this juncture, the theological debate becomes too subtle for our purposes. The important point is that our modes of spirituality differ. The difference manifests itself in our respective liturgical practices as well. When you attend an Eastern Orthodox liturgy, try to be aware of the various ways in which the transcendence and majesty of God receive emphasis in the ritual.

Most ecumenists would claim that our differing approaches to spirituality provide no real difficulty regarding our eventual reunion. Whatever our model of unity may be, it certainly must leave room for a vast array of approaches to God. Some people think that if a person worships God in a way other than the Roman Catholics do, they are wrong. As is often the case, a look at history discounts such a blatant misconception. Coming at ecumenism from the vantage point of spirituality, we discover a fine example of what we termed in the last chapter "unity amid diversity." Part of the conversion we need to undergo continually is openness to a variety of approaches to God. The immensely rich spiritual heritage of the Eastern Orthodox Church is not something we, as Westerners, can turn our backs on. In reference to the Eastern monastic spiritual tradition, the Decree on Ecumenism urges Catholics "to avail themselves more often of these spiritual riches of the Eastern Fathers, riches which lift up the whole man to the contemplation of divine mysteries" (art. 15).

2.   The Trinity

The most sublime mystery of the Christian faith is the Trinity: there is one God of three distinct persons, Father, Son, and Holy Spirit. The continuing centrality of this doctrine is evidenced by its prominent position within Vatican II's leading document, The Dogmatic Constitution on the Church (read articles 2, 3, and 4).

While all Christians are united in regard to this basic doctrine, a great diversity of theological discussion legitimately exists in our efforts to express such an ineffable mystery. One of the barriers between Roman Catholics and Orthodox Catholics, which most Orthodox regard as the major doctrinal issue, is the phrase *filioque* in the doctrine of the Trinity.

The issue can be found within the Nicene Creed, used at Mass. This creed was originally used by Christians in Jerusalem in the 4th century. After it was approved at the Ecumenical Council of Constantinople in 381, it gained wide acceptance in both the East and the West. In this creed, the Spirit is said to proceed from the Father. However, in Spain, an addition was made in which the Spirit is said to proceed from the Father and the Son. The Latin word for "and the son" is *filioque*. In the West, the use of *filioque* became more widespread, while in the East it was considered to be heretical. The real problem arises from the fact that *filioque* was officially added to the creed by Rome in 1014 without ever consulting the East. This is another example of an unnecessary wall between East and West. Most theologians today would admit that this dispute over *filioque* has some importance but is not an irreversible dogma that should hinder reunion between the two churches.

The distinction here between theological theory and dogma is an important one for ecumenical relations, and the *filioque* controversy is but one of many instances in which we must examine the relationship between the two. Insofar as *filioque* is officially part of our creed, defined at a Council, one might claim that it is dogmatic, or binding, on all those who would profess the true faith. But when we examine the historical circumstances under which *filioque* was added to the creed, then the suspicion arises that the line between theological theory and dogma cannot be drawn too rigidly and neatly. The addition of *filioque* can be said to be, after careful examination, historically conditioned. That is to say, at one time in history it constituted an addition to Catholic dogma that was truly significant for some people, in some places. Today, however, in fresh historical circumstances, it does not ultimately matter whether one hold it or not, and so it belongs in the realm of theological theory.

This is precisely what the Council Fathers had in mind when in the Decrèe on Ecumenism they stated that there exists a certain "hierarchy" of truths (art. 11), a phrase which the great German theologian Karl Rahner suggested was one of the most important of the whole Council. The Decree very wisely does not define precisely what the "hierarchy" consists of, that is, which truths are essential and which are non-essential. This is one of many instances in which what a document does not say is as important as what it does say. As a result, room is left open for the churches to work together, cautiously, in deciding those essential truths which one day will bind us together as one family and those many areas of belief and practice where there is so much room for legitimate diversity.

3. Ecumenical Councils

You might take a moment to look over a time line that lists all of the ecumenical councils of the Catholic Church. We already considered what the word "ecumenical" implied in relation to councils, and we have also discussed the history of the gradual estrangement of the two churches. In light of this knowledge, what attitude do you think the East has concerning the so-called "ecumenical" councils after the end of the first millenium? As you can probably conclude, the East would consider these later councils as valid local or regional gatherings for the Western Church but would certainly not consider them ecumenical (that is, binding on them, since they did not participate). From the Eastern perspective, it took a certain audacity on the part of the West to call their councils ecumenical. The Eastern Orthodox consider only the first seven councils as binding.

Most ecumenical theologians would not insist that the East accept all of the councils of the West. Rather, the councils of the second millennium could be viewed as "synods" or "general councils" of the Western church, that is, they would not be seen as ecumenical in nature (not binding on anyone except Western Catholics). Furthermore, there is the growing realization that these later councils focused on problems that are limited in scope and apply to particular historical circumstances—historically conditioned, to recall the term used above. Thus, there is no reason to force them onto the Eastern Church.

The Major Difference   The issues we have discussed so far are not permanent obstacles to reunion. But the problem of the papacy seems to be the greatest barrier. Not only is it a problem in dialogue between the Orthodox and Roman Catholic Churches, but it is also a problem in the various other dialogues as we shall discuss in future chapters. There are many who believe that once this problem is solved, nearly all other issues will "fall into place." Unfortunately, the debate on the papacy offers no easy solution. And the eventual solution remains buried—more so on this issue than on any other—beneath bias, resentment, and misunderstanding on all sides. Since the problem looms so large, it is best to devote a whole section to it at this early point in our journey through the various dialogues.

Infallibility   First, it is necessary to distinguish infallibility and primacy, both of which were proclaimed dogmatically at Vatican I in 1869-70. Infallibility refers to matters of doctrine, to the realm of teaching concerning faith (what we believe) and morals (how we should act). Primacy refers to jurisdiction or government, that is, matters like naming bishops or setting church policies where no doctrine of the faith is at stake. The two are "twin dogmas" insofar as they combine to give the pope supreme authority in the church. Our discussion will begin by focusing on infallibility.

The question is often asked, "Why is the dogma of infallibility even needed?" The usual argument against it is that since all human beings make mistakes, the claim of infallibility for anyone is pure arrogance. But let us carefully uncover, in several steps, the reasoning behind infallibility. Notice that as we go through the steps, if any one step is not accepted, then the whole line of reasoning fails. Step one: We begin with the conviction that God does in fact reveal himself to man. God is not merely the "prime mover" of the universe who creates and then abandons. Step two: When God does reveal himself, that revelation is considered to be of utmost importance. Step three: God is infinitely wise, and therefore would not transmit revelation without some kind of safeguard to protect the message from error. Step four: God therefore grants this needed protection by guaranteeing infallibility, that is, a promise that error will not occur in important matters of the church's teaching.

One might easily accept the reasoning of the first three steps, but upon arrival at the fourth, the real questions begin. Notice, though, the intentional vagueness of the last step. Who does God endow with infallibility? Your first response may well be, "the pope," and that is what causes so many problems in our ecumenical dialogues. It may come as a shock to realize, however, that infallibility was never considered to reside first and foremost with the pope. Papal infallibility is secondary to what we can term ecclesial infallibility. This second type means that the whole church, working together, is infallible. Let us carefully consider exactly what Vatican I had to say:

> And so...We, with the approval of the sacred council, teach and define that it is divinely revealed dogma: that the Roman Pontiff, when he speaks *ex cathedra* (that is when, acting in the office of the shepherd and teacher of all Christians, he defines by virtue of his supreme authority, doctrine concerning faith or morals to be held by the universal church), possesses through the divine assistance promised to him in the person of St. Peter, the infallibility with which the divine Redeemer willed his church to be endowed in defining doctrine concerning faith or morals....

Two points can be made in light of this. 1) The infallibility of the pope is placed within the context of the infallibility of the whole believing community. The pope has that infallibility with which Christ "willed his church to be endowed." Thus, the pope speaks infallibly when he acts as the mouthpiece of the entire church. The pope serves the church by leading it and speaking for it. 2) There are limits to the infallibility of the pope. He is not infallible in regard to his own theological views, his opinions about politics, his comments to tourists. Rather, he is infallible when he speaks *ex cathedra* (literally, "from the chair"), voicing for the church doctrine concerning faith and morals. This correction of popular opinion has profound implications in our quest for unity, as we shall continue to discuss.

There is really only one instance in which the pope has proclaimed an infallible dogma since Vatican I: The Assumption of the Blessed Virgin Mary in 1953. The dogma of the Immaculate Conception was proclaimed in 1854 before Vatican I but also reflects the only other explicit *ex cathedra* definition. There is widespread disagreement as to whether or not other papal pronouncements are endowed with some degree of infallibility. While Catholics are asked to assent to magisterial pronouncements, these are not unchanging infallible dogmas. They are better viewed as strongly needed guidelines for us. There are a number of instances in history in which magisterial positions have, in fact, changed when a new cultural epoch emerged.

Primacy of the Pope   While infallibility has to do with matters of faith and morals, primacy has to do with the practical matters of government and discipline within the church. With Vatican I, the pope's primacy of jurisdiction tended to go toward unhealthy extremes, giving the church a governmental structure that can best be described as rigidly monarchical. We have seen how Vatican II encouraged the use of other models (mystery, pilgrim) to balance this institutional model. But we must consider this monarchically centralizing tendency in the proper historical perspective. Rome was, in a sense, under "siege" by the surrounding culture and thus reacted defensively so as to preserve the truth entrusted to her. For example, the Age of Enlightenment (beginning c. 1750) virtually removed revelation and faith and substituted human reason. Mankind had "come of age" and, supposedly, no longer needed faith in God. The intellect could provide answers to the mysteries of the universe. At the time of the French Revolution (1789), authoritative structures and clericalism were extremely suspect. These and a myriad of other factors undermined the legacy of the church. The natural tendency on the part of the church was to become centralized and unified so as to retain identity and cohesiveness amid rapidly changing cultural conditions. The defensiveness of the church is understandable and can be appreciated in light of the fact that she must witness to eternal, unchanging truths in the flux of cultural growth and the confusion that comes with it.

The church continued to act defensively against the on-slaught of modern culture for nearly a century after Vatican I. For example, many new and valuable forms of scholarship and historical inquiry were developed in the wake of Enlightenment thinking. Scholars were increasingly using these indispensable critical tools in their examination and reassessment of the Bible and church tradition. In 1907, the church officially condemned such innovation, labeling it "modernism." Later, the church would move from its extremely preservationist attitude and make room for transformation, allowing her scholars to use the new methods of inquiry.

In this historical context, it is easy to understand how Catholics accepted a very centralistic and authoritative interpretation of the papacy. The pope was the "general," so to speak, leading Catholicism in its war against modern culture. Catholics increasingly went to the extreme of leading their lives simply by doing what they were told to do, adopting almost a military discipline. Many of the subtleties in Vatican I's definition of infallibility were ignored, leading to the conviction that "the pope is infallible." As we have seen, it is not quite that simple.

Vatican II and the Papacy   Vatican II brought with it a radical shift in mindset, examples of which we have already seen. In the Pastoral Constitution on the Church in the Modern World, modern culture was no longer seen as an enemy, but rather as an important partner in dialogue. The church saw that she could no longer simply block herself off from a rapidly changing world; the time was ripe to come to terms with emerging forms of thought and culture. The church had to formulate her universal and unchanging truth in a fresh way, in new modes of expression that would meet new needs. She had to reinterpret many doctrines in a revitalized way. This is precisely what Vatican II did in regard to papal primacy and infallibility. On the one hand, it affirmed Vatican I's teaching. But on the other hand, it reinterpreted the doctrine by making some important clarifications and emphasizing certain points that had been overlooked in the previous century.

The new emphasis regarding the papacy can be described under three basic principles. First, we find a revitalization of the principle of collegiality. This means that a new stress is placed on the entire college of bishops who represent all of the local churches. Thus, we find a shift from a monarchical view to a collegial view in which there is a real sharing of powers and duties. Lay people working in their parishes can influence priests, who can in turn influence the local bishops, who can in turn influence the pope. Thus, with Vatican II, there is a real sense of all of us working together to make decisions. Of course, the process is slow, and changes occur only gradually. But the shift in emphasis is there and the process should not be underestimated as mere lip service. As Raymond Brown, a biblical scholar committed to ecumenism, has pointed out:

> Once such consultative bodies have been introduced, eventually they have an effect. No human relationship is possible if the person who makes the decision consistently vetoes the advice of the group he consults...a collegial force is at work, and the machinery for consultation is in place; eventually they will broaden the decision-making process (*Critical Meaning of the Bible*, p.116).

This collegial force is rooted in The Dogmatic Constitution of the Church, the leading document from Vatican II. Chapter Two is entitled "The People of God" and serves as the setting within which subsequent chapters on the hierarchy and laity develop. This is a classic example of the depth of vision that is so manifest in the documents of the Council.

A second shift of emphasis, one we have already discussed, can be seen in the principle of unity amid legitimate diversity. According to this principle, there can be a real plurality of theologies, spiritualities, laws and customs within a church unified by common essentials that are continually expressed and re-expressed by the papacy. We spoke of a plurality of spiritualities earlier—why can there not be a genuine plurality in many other areas as well? Certain communities may have needs that are quite distinctive from those of other communities. Article 16 of the Decree on Ecumenism makes this precise point in reference to the Eastern Churches:

From the earliest times...the Eastern Churches followed their own disciplines, sanctioned by the holy Fathers, by synods, even by ecumenical councils. Far from being an obstacle to the church's unity, such diversity of customs and observances only adds to her comeliness, and contributes greatly to carrying out her mission....To remove any shadow of doubt, then, this sacred Synod solemnly declares that the churches of the East, while keeping in mind the necessary unity of the whole church, have the power to govern themselves according to their own disciplines, since these are better suited to the temperament of their faithful and better adapted to foster the good of souls. Although it has not always been honored, the strict observance of this traditional principle is among the prerequisites for any restoration of unity.

Thus, diversity is not something that we are now asked to tolerate; rather, it is an essential feature of a church that is truly catholic.

Some might argue that such diversity implies separation. On the other hand, though, the papacy can provide a real sense of cohesiveness while at the same time allowing for a great deal of diversity. Many are convinced that stubbornness on the part of Roman Catholics concerning their view of the papacy is primarily responsible for stunting the otherwise promising growth toward unity. However, the ability of the papacy to be a unifying force amid great diversity is essential for making greater strides toward ecumenical union. This could be, paradoxically, one of the key Roman Catholic contributions to the future ecumenical union of Christians.

Of course, this "papal contribution" has to come from a papacy renewed along the lines we have just described. This renewal will be enhanced by a consideration of some of the jurisdiction practices of the Eastern Orthodox tradition. For example, the Patriarch of Constantinople is considered to have what is called a primacy of honor, which strikes a different tone than does the primacy of jurisdiction which the Western church inherited following Vatican I. The Patriarch of Constantinople is considered to be "first among equals," serving the cause of unity among the Orthodox, but at the same time allowing diverse local churches to flourish. Is it toward this model that the papacy should move? We must remember that while we are committed to the papacy, we need not be committed to any one form of it, which can and does change throughout history.

Finally, a third shift of emphasis can be found in the principle of subsidiarity, which has to do with how we view the structure of the institutional church. Catholics have been accustomed to seeing the church as a pyramid. At the top is the pope, and toward the bottom we find all of the local churches, and finally the individual members. The principle of subsidiarity means that the emphasis changes, and we view the church from the bottom up. To begin with, the people are the essential part of the church. Our local congregations are the core, the center, of the church. The papacy, no longer monopolistic, is crucial insofar as it serves the unity of all local churches.

The fears of those who feel such changes in emphasis betray the centuries-old tradition of the church can be calmed by a look to history. The three shifts of emphasis we have described are actually a return to the ecclesiology (way of looking at the church) of the first millenium. It is a return to what we could term a "communion ecclesiology": The church is a communion of local churches and the bishops of the local churches exercise a more complete jurisdictional authority. The pope acts as a servant to the cause of unity, strengthening all the local churches in their one, united faith in Jesus Christ. As the Decree on Ecumenism reminds us:

> For many centuries, the churches of the East and of the West went their own ways, though a brotherly communion of faith and sacramental life bound them together. If disagreements in belief and discipline arose among them, the Roman See acted by common consent as moderator (art.14).

Orthodox/Roman Catholic Dialogue   What does our dialogue with the Orthodox Church look like? The two leaders of Rome and Constantinople are again in close communication—oriented toward reunion. In 1965, toward the end of Vatican II, Pope Paul VI and Patriarch Athenagoras nullified the excommunications of 1054 in ceremonies at both Rome and Istanbul. Other gestures have followed.

For example, in 1965, a bilateral commission was formed in the United States. Having met approximately twenty times so far, it has issued seven "consensus statements" in which the two theological teams were able to reach genuine agreement. These statements, which are good sources for future exploration, deal with topics such as the eucharist, the sanctity of marriage, mixed marriages, respect for life, and the church. At an ecumenical commemoration of the Second Council of Constantinople in 1981 in Rome, Pope John Paul II prayed the Constantinopolitan Creed in its original form without the *filioque*.

On the worldwide level, great progress has been made as well. Commissions were established on both sides in 1975 to prepare for theological dialogue. The precise results of these commissions remain an open question. The key point is that, despite the obstacles, there is genuine interest on both sides for reunion.

Once again, though, we must realize that the greatest obstacles remain within all of us as individuals. While theologians and members of the hierarchy gather in commissions for discussion, we must individually commit ourselves to becoming educated about each other's history and beliefs in a warm and genuine spirit of openness to one another. That calls for real conversion.

Before we end this chapter, and for the sake of completeness, it is important to point out that there are Eastern Catholic Churches as well as Eastern Orthodox Churches. Beginning in the sixteenth century and developing in the seventeenth and eighteenth centuries, small groups of Eastern Christians entered into full communion with Rome, accepting papal primacy but maintaining the integrity of their legitimate Eastern Christian approach to spirituality, history, and liturgical customs. Thus, today there are representatives of every Christian liturgical family within the Catholic Church.

These churches are in an uncomfortable situation. They are unlike the "majority" Roman rite Catholics, and they are often alienated from the Orthodox Churches because of their acceptance of papal primacy. Roman Catholics should be aware of this and supportive of these communities. Only by study, listening, and reflection can we appreciate the richness of liturgical families within the community of faith.

QUESTIONS
FOR REFLECTION AND DISCUSSION

1. How has a sense of history affected your views of 1) Early theological disputes; 2) Differences in Christian religious practice; 3) The Great Schism?

2. Should the message of Jesus be closely identified with any particular culture?

3. What kind of attitude is needed for divergent cultures to get along together?

4. What are some truths that you believe are essential to bind all Christians together?

5. What are some beliefs or practices that Christians might disagree about but still be united?

6. How do you envision that disputes will be resolved in a more pluralistic church?

7. Do you feel that the Roman Catholic Church should become a member of the World Council of Churches?

8. What are the popular conceptions about papal infallibility?

9. Why do you feel there is so much ecumenical concern about infallibility?

10. What do you understand to be the distinction between the Orthodox "primacy of honor" and the Roman Catholic "primacy of jurisdiction"?

11. Which reforms of Vatican II do you think have best indicated the church's desire for unity?

12. Do you feel that the Orthodox or Roman Catholics must make some concessions before there can be unity?

13. When do you think that reunion between the Eastern and Western Churches will take place?

CHAPTER FIVE

The
Lutheran
Tradition

Lutheranism was originally intended to be a reform or renewal movement within the Catholic Church, strengthening it in its divine mission. It tried to pinpoint areas in which the human side of the church had fallen into error and to do something about it. It was never meant to cause disunity. In the Augsburg Confession of 1530, written a short time after Luther's initial challenge to the church, we find a plea to both sides "to have all of us embrace and adhere to a single, true religion and live together in unity in one fellowship and church, even as we all enlisted under one Christ." This document contains the central thrust, the key insights, of the original reformers. So fundamental is the document that Lutheranism can also be termed "The Church of the Augsburg Confession."

It is well known, of course, that the unity requested in the Augsburg Confession never took place. Instead, due to the apologetical and polemical atmosphere of the sixteenth century, the most divisive event in the history of the church began to take place, the Protestant Reformation. What might have strengthened the church in her mission to unify the human family instead weakened her more than ever before. Today, converted to a more ecumenical mindset, Lutherans and Roman Catholics can look back to the original intent of the reform movement with a more mature attitude and begin to take concrete steps—ones that should have been taken right from the start—toward unity.

In many ways the Lutheran/Catholic dialogue is the most promising ecumenical event taking place today. Critics have held it up as a model for other dialogue groups to emulate. As a result of a long series of bilateral discussions spearheaded by the best in Roman Catholic and Lutheran scholarship, six consensus statements have been drawn up. The discussions reveal that Roman Catholics and Lutherans are surprisingly close to each other, especially since many of the problems Luther originally confronted have now been resolved within the Roman Catholic Church. Differences do remain, but there is an openness to pluralism and genuine unity—amid legitimate differences that are no longer insurmountable. Also, the reformers retained a great deal of the traditions of the first fifteen centuries of the church, which gives both groups a common basis to work on. Four hundred and fifty years after the original split, there is good reason to hope that the breach can be mended, the scars healed.

Roots of the Reformation   In more recent times, the Roman Catholic Church has been blessed with capable and devoted pontiffs. However, in the centuries preceding the Reformation, the papacy was in an unfortunate and deplorable state of decline. In part, this was due to the bad influence of the more "pagan" elements of the Age of Renaissance: indulgence in wealth, power, and "good living." For example, from 1378 to 1417 there existed a dual claim to the papacy; one "pope" resided in Rome and the other in Avignon, France. Later, there were three rival popes who all excommunicated one another and sought their own exclusive group of followers. Alexander VI, perhaps the worst leader in the history of the church, was pope during Martin Luther's early years.

In addition to these papal difficulties, the leadership of the church behaved in ways almost unimaginable to us today. The popes sold leadership posts in the church to the highest bidders, or they gave them to their friends or relatives. In order to support their luxurious standard of living, they engaged in the practice of selling indulgences and relics of the saints. The parish clergy accepted large sums of money for their services. Superstitious and magical practices became commonplace. For example, the faithful were encouraged to buy indulgences and thus be assured of a shorter stay in purgatory. They were encouraged to gaze at the host to assure immunity from tragic occurrences. Thus some people tried to attend several masses a day and even bribed the priest to hold the host up longer. A tragic and unfortunate amount of poor leadership and just plain ignorance led to such abuses. The stage was set for a thorough renewal in the church.

In 1517, a monk named Johann Tetzel visited Wittenberg, Germany, to collect funds for the building of St. Peter's in Rome. To raise money, he sold indulgences. This outraged Martin Luther, also a monk, who believed that God's grace could not be purchased. He decided to fight this and other abuses. In 1519, in accord with the practices of the time, he nailed his famous "95 Theses" to the church door in Wittenberg, indicating that he wanted to engage in public debate. This was only the beginning of Luther's long struggle against the abuses of the church, a struggle inspired by an intense desire for renewal, not for separation. What were essential ideas behind Luther's quest for renewal? Primarily, the question of justification.

A basic theme of the New Testament is that God has reconciled the world to himself; in Christ, God destroyed the barriers which human sin, particularly pride, had erected between humanity and divinity. This barrier was caused by the sin or fall of our first parents, a sin of disobedience and pride, which we inherit as original sin. Christ's redemption reconciled us to God. Although we retain our inborn tendency to rebel against God in a variety of sinful ways, at the same time we can be confident that despite our sinfulness, we are loved and cared for by God—we are reconciled to or justified before God. This justification is a free gift to us from God. There is nothing we can do to merit it. We must rely totally on God.

As Luther saw it, Tetzel and other representatives of the hierarchy made forgiveness and reconciliation (justification), dependent on individual acts of piety or on monetary donations instead of on God. He felt that it was an act of pride for the church to set up her own human standards for determining who was justified before God. In other words, the church had, perhaps inadvertently, erected barriers between God and humanity. She had developed what she considered means for helping believers in their relationship with God. But these means too often became ends in themselves. Believers relied on them for their assurance of salvation, rather than relying on God.

Thus, Luther was reacting against abusive forms of mediation between God and humanity. Some Protestant preachers would later reject all forms of mediation, forgetting that they can be helpful when used correctly. Roman Catholics had indeed gone to the other extreme by allowing superstitious and magical practices to be considered mediation. A balanced view was necessary.

We believe that our relationship with God can, of course, be mediated or aided through the sacraments, through the Scriptures, or through good preaching. But we must always be on guard, as Luther was, against allowing those forms of mediation to become ends in themselves, thinking that something we "do" makes us acceptable to God. Luther correctly saw that the sin of pride was taking over in Catholic practice. Various institutional elements such as the papacy, the sacraments, or devotions could stand between humans and God in a destructive way, making persons subject to and dependent on these worldly realities instead of on God, first and foremost. According to the Augsburg Confession, "...men cannot be justified before God by their own strength, merits, or works, but are freely justified for Christ's sake, through faith..." (art. IV).

Luther's Struggle   In order to understand and appreciate Luther's focus on total dependence upon God, it is helpful to examine his life situation. Luther was a man with an exceptionally sensitive conscience and he was spiritually intense

almost constantly. We have all experienced times of spiritual
intensity in our lives during which we examine ourselves before
God, asking ourselves such ultimate questions as: "Have I made
the best choice?" "Am I living up to my potential?" "How well
am I meeting the difficult demands of my faith?" Often we
are driven to such questioning when we experience our own
weaknesses, our limitations, our sinfulness. Luther was plagued
by his own weakness and sinfulness and was very in tune with
the evil and depraved dimensions of human existence. For him,
the ultimate question was "How can I be saved?" His constant
desire was to please and be one with God, to gain eternal
happiness; yet his constant fear was that he fell short, due to
his own innate weakness and sinfulness.

The initial way in which Luther tried to answer his question was monasticism, which was then considered the ideal
way of Christian life. But despite his exceptionally diligent pur-
suit of the religious life, his sense of sin and failure persisted.
The more he tried to find peace, it seemed, the more frustrated
he became. The church assured believers that through the sacrament of Confession, they were guaranteed forgiveness and
could find peace. But this did not satisfy Luther. At the heart
of his difficulty was the fact that human sinfulness lay deeper
than specific offenses. Human nature was corrupted as a result
of Original Sin, and so human nature itself stood in need of
transformation. Luther was keenly aware that he was helpless
in the face of this needed transformation. There was nothing
he could do, on his own, to be accepted by God.

Luther's solution came suddenly one night as he was
preparing lectures in the tower of the monastery. He read in
Saint Paul's letter to the Romans that "the just man lives by
faith." He concluded that, since there is nothing we can do
to earn acceptance, only the grace of God that comes through
faith can justify us. Thus, we have the famous dictum "justification by grace through faith." Each person remains a sinner;
there is still an essential flaw in human nature, but simultaneously the person is justified by God in view of Christ's
atonement. Such justification is communicated to each of us
through our faith in God's redemptive love. Thus, for Luther,
the person is *simul justus et peccator*, simultaneously justified

and sinful. With this paradox—the pain of knowing one is sinful and the joy of knowing one is still acceptable—we must live out our lives.

Recovering God's Word as Authoritative   We've already seen that Luther wanted to peel away what he considered "excess baggage"—those things that obstructed the path to God. For Luther, the believer's own experience of justification before God was of ultimate concern. No external power or system (the pope or church tradition) had the right to impose itself on the individual in relationship to God. Thus, the individual believer is not under the authority of the pope, or an intricate system of sacramental rubrics. He considered these human elements to be barriers between people and God. This is quite understandable, considering the state of the Catholic Church in Luther's time.

Luther replaced the authority of man-made tradition with the authority of God's word, which is a living and vital reality. It is discovered in Scripture, and thus we encounter Luther's famous *dictum sola scriptura* (by Scripture alone). He believed that God's word could be mediated through sound preaching. A good preacher, having reflected carefully on the Scriptures, would be like the mouthpiece of God, bringing the living word to the heart of individual believers. Such preaching was noticeably missing in the Catholic practices of Luther's time.

Since the word of God alone is authoritative, no set of individual believers has any special authority that might put them in a privileged position. Clericalism was rampant in Luther's time, as we have seen. Luther replaced the "hierarchy" with the "priesthood of all believers." Everyone was on equal footing: all were sinful, all were in need of justification.

Centuries later, an important ecumenical concept evolved from Luther's priesthood of all believers: No individual experience could be absolutized or held up as authoritative. Respect for each person's distinct and diverse experience has been called the "Protestant Principle," which also recognizes the importance of objective truth handed down vis-a-vis tradition. Protestantism inevitably developed authoritative traditions of its own, for without such structures, its churches would be without substance. And likewise, Catholicism has never negated the value or validity of individual religious experience. Catholic unity has always been predicated on diversity.

Unfortunately, Luther's important contributions have been blurred for centuries because of the polemical positions that arose for which both sides are to blame. But today, Roman Catholics can and must rediscover Luther. The best way to begin this process is through a careful reading of the Augsburg Confession. This document embraces the essence of Luther's original plea for renewal.

In 1521, Luther was excommunicated by the pope and declared outside the law. But his request for renewal had resonated positively in the hearts of many people. He attracted thousands of followers as well as the protection of his ruler, the Elector of Saxony. However, polemical positions began to harden on all sides and disunity was becoming apparent. A political situation caused the leaders to come to terms with this disunity. The Holy Roman Empire was being threatened militarily by the Turks, who, having already occupied most of Hungary, were now laying siege to Vienna. Emperor Charles V saw that in this situation, unity among the people of Germany was crucial. He convened the Diet of Augsburg in 1530 in an attempt to unify the Empire by settling religious differences. For this occasion, Philip Melanchthon penned the Augsburg Confession as a theological summary of the reformer's views and a plea for unity.

The Confession is divided into two basic parts. The first part consists of 21 articles that deal with the doctrine of the triune God, human sinfulness, Christology, justification, good works, the church and its ministry, and the sacraments. The reformers emphasized here that they were in essential agreement with the Catholic faith: "...our churches dissent in no article of the faith from the Catholic Church...."

The second part of the Confession deals with changes that were necessary to counter abuse. Change and renewal based on Scripture are common threads that run through the Confession.

Article XXII, for example, urges that the laity receive Communion under both species at the Lord's Supper, on the basis of appeal to Scripture and early church tradition. Gradually the church had developed the custom of distributing the bread alone. But this was only a custom, and as such was not eternally binding. Today, Catholic tradition has in fact changed the custom and also returned to the more biblical pattern. Some, however, still confuse this custom with an immutable doctrine of faith.

Article XXIII deals with the custom of priestly celibacy. This issue arose out of several historical circumstances. Scandals were apparently common concerning priests who were not leading chaste lives. In addition, there existed bitter memories of priests who, originally having been allowed to marry, later had the law of celibacy imposed on them. And so the reformers wished to return to a more biblical pattern in which there was apparently, according to scriptural evidence available, no law of celibacy for priests. The Roman Catholic position is that the tradition of celibacy is a development guided by the Holy Spirit, and as such is binding on all clergy. It was at councils held during the fourth century that the law became definite.

The difference in opinion can best be handled by realizing that both Roman Catholic and Lutheran practices or customs are legitimate and both have intrinsic value. The value of married priests, in part, is that the priesthood is accessible to many more people whose competence can be utilized. On the other hand, there exists a real value in priestly celibacy, as our tradition attests, which ought never to be lost.

Thus, while the Roman Catholic tradition needs to continue opening up more roles of service for married people, and while such roles might eventually be given a clerical status, as in the Lutheran communion, a special and highly respected place ought always to be reserved for those who choose to serve as celibates.

Abuses discussed in the second part of the Augsburg Confession include extreme power for bishops (who had increasingly moved their sphere of influence into civil affairs, often to the detriment of their spiritual ministry), monastic vows (a wide variety of abuses had entered into the monastic life-style), and distortions existing in the Mass.

Through the Augsburg Confession, the Lutherans wanted to demonstrate that they were loyal to the Catholic Church and not interested in beginning a schism. The Confession showed a willingness on the part of the reformers to compromise for the sake of unity while remaining a source of renewal in the church. Unfortunately, the two sides were unable to agree. A schism was not what Martin Luther had in mind when he first began to seek renewal within the church, but he considered it preferable to simply acquiescing to the un-Christian abuses which were so prevalent.

Now 450 years after the Augsburg Confession, when we compare the reforms asked for in that document to the reforms that are taking place in the post-Vatican II church, we find an amazing similarity. Together, the documents from Vatican II and the Augsburg Confession can serve as texts upon which solid ecumenical foundations can be laid. Both sides are now demonstrating an authentic ecumenical attitude, and the dialogues that have taken place are quite promising. In the United States alone, there have been seven rounds of discussions covering these topics: 1) the creed, 2) baptism, 3) eucharist, 4) ministry, 5) papal primacy, 6) teaching authority, and 7) infallibility and justification.

The Papacy: Some Current Perspectives   As we have seen, the abuses taking place in the hierarchy of the church and the papacy initially prompted Luther's call for reform. Pope Boniface VIII, in *Unan Sanctum* (1302), had contended that in order to obtain salvation, every human creature must be subject to the Roman pontiff. Such a claim is understandable given the historical circumstances: Boniface's pontificate marked the summit of over a century of tremendous and positive influence on the part of the papacy. But this "summit" turned out to be a precipice over which papal influence was to plunge. The escalating abuses gave Luther reason to protest, convinced that justification cannot depend on any particular institutional structure of the church. While Luther initially wanted to reform the papacy, the end result was a flat-out rejection of it. We have seen how the Augsburg Confession failed to find mutual acceptance on both sides. The frustration of the reformers was apparent when, seven years later Luther wrote the *Smalcald Articles* which included an exceptionally harsh criticism of the papacy. Luther contended that the papacy was a mere human institution and that it was not willed by God. In fact, he went so far as to claim that the pope was the anti-Christ and that Christians ought not be subject to his tyrannical authority. The papacy, as Luther saw it, puts its own requirements for salvation in place of God's free giving of the same without any requirements.

On the Roman Catholic side, the Lutheran position was considered an attack on the unity of the one, true church. However, the Church of Rome began to realize that many of the abuses would have to be corrected. To this end, the Council of Trent was convened in 1545 after much delay caused by quarrelling between the pope and the emperor. Partly, the quarrel had to do with whether the Council could in some way include dialogue with Protestants with hope of reconciliation. This possibility was never actualized. The bulk of the decision-making was done in the first two years of the Council, which minimized any future hope for dialogue. Progress was then delayed by an epidemic and then by the death of Pope Paul III. The Council reconvened on and off until 1563, but hope for reconciliation was further minimized by increased feuding among various Catholic factions. Besides, the Peace of Augsburg in 1555 gave Protestants civil equality with Catholics, giving them more of a basis on which to maintain their separate identity.

The tragedy of the Council of Trent is that it started reform too late to prevent the disastrous rift. It is truly unfortunate that Luther's insights and quest for renewal could not have existed within the institutional church. For this, as the Decree on Ecumenism stated, both sides are to blame.

Closing the Gap   Without the apologetical and polemical atmosphere of the sixteenth century the two sides are closer today than ever before concerning the papacy. Many of the original Lutheran objections have been answered as Roman

Catholicism has gradually employed the following three principles. 1) There must be the realization that unity does not re-
quire absolute uniformity, that "...a variety of ecclesial types
should never foster divisiveness" (Dialogue V, p.20, Papal
Primacy and The Universal Church). In other words, the two
sides do not have to completely agree in every area of custom,
law, liturgy, spirituality, etc. The Augsburg Confession suggests this same principle: "It is not necessary for the true unity
of the Christian church that ceremonies, instituted by men,
should be observed uniformly in all places" (art. VII). 2)
Authority needs to be understood as being more collegial than
monarchial. As the dialogue on this topic states, "No one person or administrative staff, however indicated, learned, and
experienced, can grasp all the subtleties and complexities of
situations in a world-wide church, whose many communities
live and bear witness in the variegated contexts of several con-
tinents and many nations" (V:20 Papal Primacy...). 3) Subsidiarity must be practiced more widely. As we view the church
more and more from the "bottom up," we ourselves must
become more responsible:

> What can properly be decided and done in smaller units of
> ecclesial life ought not be referred to church leaders who have
> wider responsibilities. Decisions should be made and activities
> carried out with a participation as broad as possible from the
> people of God. Initiatives should be encouraged in order to pro-
> mote a wholesome diversity in theology, worship, witness, and
> service (ibid.).

If these principles of reform continue to be applied to the
papacy, the original Lutheran hopes for a reformed papacy
could eventually be fulfilled. On the Lutheran side, there must
be the recognition that some ministry of overseeing church
unity everywhere is necessary for there to be true unity—the
"Catholic contribution." The Lutheran participants in the
theological dialogues that stated: "We cannot responsibly dis-
miss the possibility that some form of the papacy, renewed
and restructured under the gospel, may be an appropriate expression of the ministry that serves the unity and ordering of
the church" (V:20). Lutherans can profitably look to the ways

in which Roman Catholics today, after Vatican II, are in relationship with the pope. On some issues there exists conflict between respect for authority and the following of one's conscience. But the pope and the bishops seem to be "pastorally tolerant," in Raymond Brown's words of the resulting diversity. Likewise, the faithful tend to be sympathetic rather than hostile toward a magisterium that has the challenging task of speaking to a worldwide church in all its facets (Cf, Brown, *Critical Meaning of the Bible*, p.118). And one must recognize that in many very important issues (essential doctrines, the need for justice and peace, the need for unity) the pope does, in fact, voice the common vision of all the faithful and serves the church as a unifying force of inestimable value.

An essential part of the move toward unity, of course, is eliminating some of the misunderstandings between Lutherans and Catholics. A prime example of misunderstanding is infallibility. Lutherans have felt that the doctrine undercuts the unique role of Jesus Christ and Scripture by placing the Pope above them—thus, Luther's *dictum sola scriptura*. The Second Vatican Council was careful to clarify this issue when it stated that the papacy is not above the word of God, but rather serves it, by listening to it, guarding it, and explaining it (On Revelation, art.10). On the other hand, Roman Catholics have felt that Lutherans never trusted enough that God would faithfully guide the church and protect it from error. However, Lutherans did not initially lack in trust that God would steer the church on right paths; rather, Luther wanted greater trust in God instead of in a human institution that had fallen into abuse. He ended up rejecting an institution that is necessary for true unity. Today, though, that institution is placed within its proper perspective, as serving the word of God which alone is infallible. From this perspective, all sides can reconsider the benefits of a central figure who serves the unity of the church.

Sharing Key Beliefs   Roman Catholics and Lutherans are slowly beginning to realize that we are much closer to one another than we had ever imagined. The basis for such essential closeness is that we both share the same creed. A creed is a carefully formulated statement that expresses the essential foundations of what we believe. To realize that we both share this essential foundation is quite freeing because it means that our discussions start in the same place rather than at polar points from which we try to converge.

When two groups accept a common creed, much more is at stake than a simple agreement about abstract principles. Common faith in a creed means mutual acceptance at a much deeper level. It means that together we trust in the same God: a God who is both transcendent and immanent, who created us, loves us, and saves us. We share in the same hope that our gracious God can restore and renew with us our broken world, and the hope that being saved, we will one day see God face to face and be unified with God and one another in eternal happiness. And we believe together that out of our common faith and hope must flow a genuine love for one another. Finally, together we praise the same triune God who is the well-spring of our common faith, hope, and love. These are truly fundamental convictions about life, convictions that reach centuries back into the richness of our common Christian tradition.

Let us go back for a moment into our tradition and consider the historical origins of the creed we share. It must first be noted that the creed does not appear in Scripture as such. Scripture presents truth to us in the literary forms of stories and parables, hymns and poetry, myths and epics with deep symbolic content with only occasional formulations of the faith. Truth in these forms appeals to our affective or "feeling oriented" side (often termed "heart"). The creed takes the truth revealed to us by God and puts it in a more organized form, with more technical language. As such, it appeals more to our cognitive or rational side. Studies of the brain indicate that one side controls our affective functions and the other our cognitive functions. Different people and different cultures will invariably end up expressing themselves from one side more than the other. But both belong to us as human beings, and thus it is natural that we express the truth of revelation in both ways—affectively and cognitively.

A creed is a technical formulation or logical outline of faith. Such formulations, while essential to an organized faith, always fall short of capturing the fullness of the reality they attempt to describe. Yet, they are essential to our faith in that its expression ought to be cognitive as well as affective to reflect the fullness of the human person.

Nicaea's Response   Our creed is called the "Nicene Creed," and it takes its name from the first ecumenical Council of the church at Nicaea in 325. As you'll recall, Constantine, the emperor, called the Council in order to settle a Christological problem with Arius, who emphasized the humanity of Jesus to the exclusion of his divinity. Arius taught that Jesus did not exist co-eternally with God the Father, but rather that he was first among God's creatures. Thus, Jesus was more divine than we are, but certainly not on a par with God. If Jesus was a creature, as Arius contended, he could not be God, and therefore could not be our savior.

The Nicene Creed teaches that the Son is "eternally begotten of the Father, God from God, Light from Light, true God from true God, begotten not made, one in being with the Father." These words originated at Nicaea in order to guard against the mistake Arius had made and which others have been prone to make down through the centuries even to the present time. Notice that only by examining its historical origins does the creed really start to make sense. It gives a cognitive expression to our faith and acts as a safeguard throughout history against repeating the mistakes made in the formative years of Christianity.

The second ecumenical council took place at Constantinople in 381. At this council, the creed reached a new form when articles on the church and the Holy Spirit were added. With a few minor revisions (recall the *filioque* problem, for example), this is the creed we proclaim today. Because the final form was achieved at Constantinople, the official name of our creed is the "Nicene-Constantinopolitan Symbol." It represents several centuries of doctrinal development—that is, growth in the church's understanding—and is the creed shared by Roman Catholics, Lutherans, and Orthodox Christians today. It is truly an ecumenical creed and will serve as the foundation of our eventual reunion.

Eucharist and Liturgy   In the fourth round of the Lutheran/Roman Catholic dialogue, it was stressed that the discussion of the eucharist must never be an academic exercise alone. For the eucharist is intrinsically connected to daily life. In the eucharist, we become living sacrifices to God, and are called to take the presence of Christ into the world. This is a task that all Christians must do together; we cannot afford divisiveness among ourselves when it comes to this crucial mission. The eucharist, as such, ought to be the unifying event among all Christians. From it comes our source of life, our sustenance. Thus, our disunity is most glaring, most scandalous, when it comes to the Lord's Supper.

One difficulty today is that we inherit eucharistic differences from the time of the Reformation, differences which, as the dialogue group discovered through careful study, are no longer insurmountable. What are these basic differences? We can look to Article XXIV of the Augsburg Confession to discover them.

The Confession states that the reformers wanted very much to preserve the essence of the Mass and allow it to retain its centrality in the Christian life. Thus they defend the use of the vernacular since it allowed the faithful to better understand the Mass. Here we find a prime example of how Vatican II took to heart this needed reform, and now this problem no longer separates us. Today, most Roman Catholics have a much better understanding of exactly what is happening in the mystery of the eucharist. It is important for Catholics to note, too, that using the Latin at Mass is by no means forbidden. In fact, now that people know the meaning of the words used in the Mass, use of the original Latin at times can be quite valuable; it captures the universality of the Catholic Church, and as such it is part of our tradition that perhaps ought not be lost forever.

One of the abuses that the Confession attacked was the celebration of private Masses in exchange for a stipend, a situation that had gotten out of hand during Luther's time. Today, "private Masses" are gradually giving way to a more proper communal emphasis. As the Constitution on the Sacred Liturgy from Vatican II states:

Liturgical services are not private functions, but are celebrations of the church, which is the "sacrament of unity," namely, a holy people united and organized under their bishops (art. 26).

A misunderstanding that had developed in the church had to do with the concept of the Mass as sacrifice. Christ's death on Calvary was a once-and-for-all sacrifice that atoned for all sin. But many were under the impression that Christ had atoned for Original Sin and that individual sacrifices of the Mass were necessary to atone for our daily sins. This, too, led to a proliferation of private Masses, often said only for those who could pay the price. You can imagine how strongly Luther reacted against such a practice. For Luther, as for all Christians, our redemption is gained once and for all by Christ. We are justified not because we merit it (earn it), or pay for it by having a Mass said. Rather, we are totally dependent on God, and our justification takes place when we believe that.

Many Roman Catholics perhaps take it for granted that it is a good practice to receive Holy Communion often. This is the summit of our participation in the eucharist. Yet, in Luther's time such practice was uncommon; the Mass had become a private affair between celebrant and God, with the faithful essentially acting as spectators. The Augsburg Confession asks for a return to earlier church traditions in which communion was available to everyone. With Vatican II, the Roman Catholic Church has made this return.

Thus, we find example after example of sound ecumenism at work. Roman Catholics have preserved the essence of the eucharistic celebration—the commemoration or "making present" of Jesus Christ. At the same time, we have allowed transformation to take place. We have come to appreciate that our liturgy does not exist in one fixed, unchangeable form, but rather that change and renewal can and must take place. The essence of what we do remains the same, while the mode in which we do it is developing. While many are quite happy with the various changes that took place after the Council, others are quite displeased, and sometimes justifiably so. As we grow, we make mistakes; reacting against one extreme, we go to the other. Sometimes we end up totally abandoning the richer aspects of our liturgical tradition and only appreciate them once they are gone. The delicate interplay of preservation and transformation is indeed risky, but it is far better than a rigid and uncompromising stance. Ecumenism means that all of us can learn from one another. It is not a matter of Catholic liturgies becoming too Protestant or vice versa. We allow the form of our liturgy to grow toward its inherent richness and depth.

The primary reason why the eucharist has such depth is that we believe Christ is really present to the bread and wine. Even though both Roman Catholics and Lutherans have always affirmed this, because of misunderstandings on both sides, this has been, historically, a real point of dissension. Catholics have traditionally questioned whether Christ is really present at a Lutheran eucharist. We have accused Lutherans of treating the bread and wine as mere symbols, while they have accused us of engaging in almost magical practices regarding the elements.

Roman Catholics have traditionally used the term "transubstantiation" to express that the bread and wine are really changed, mysteriously, into Christ's body and blood. This explanation, comprising quite a complex array of philosophical subtleties, was rooted in the metaphysics of Aristotle which was recovered and put to great use in the West in the thirteenth century. The doctrine of transubstantiation was originally intended to protect the eucharist against those who would question the real presence of Christ.

Lutherans, on the other hand, found "transubstantiation" and the technical explanations of it far too rationalistic. They preferred the term "sacramental union" to express the real presence of Jesus in the bread and wine. Luther himself explained the presence of Christ using the analogy of iron and fire. When the two are combined, the fire heats and lights the iron, but both elements retain their original identity. Thus, Luther never denied the real presence. In fact, he reacted against the radical position of another reformer, Ulrich Zwingli, who held that the consecrated elements were "mere signs." Luther stressed that if he had to choose the Catholic position or Zwingli's position, he would readily take the former.

Roman Catholics and Protestants became increasingly polarized about their respective positions. Today such defensiveness is unwarranted. Both sides in the dialogue realized that the important thing is that Christ is indeed present at the eucharist. This is a mystery that we can only attempt to explain. But when one tries to express or explain a mystery one ends with a formulation that can never be fully adequate; the explanation can never completely capture or express the reality of Christ's presence. With this awareness, both sides are able to continue developing their expressions of the presence of Christ with the realization that a "perfect explanation" or one final theology is simply unattainable. Such would reduce the fullness of Christ's presence to our human and thus limited perception and explanation of it. This ecumenical attitude is a far cry from the polemically charged disagreements of the past.

A Point of Convergence   Roman Catholics and Lutherans are achieving unity in one key area of the eucharist and liturgy. We have seen how Luther was disturbed by the abuses in the Catholic tradition. Tradition, he believed, had become "man's word" getting in the way of and distorting God's word. Thus, he gave Scripture complete priority over tradition as the source of God's revelation. What were the implications of this for the liturgy?

In the Lutheran tradition, a great emphasis was placed on God's word by giving centrality to the Scripture readings and the expansion and interpretation of those readings in the sermon. Today this remains a hallmark of Lutheran services. Roman Catholics, too, have recovered the centrality of God's word in the Scriptures and in the homily. First, consider this article from the Constitution on the Sacred Liturgy:

> Sacred Scripture is of paramount importance in the celebration of the liturgy. For it is from Scripture that lessons are read and explained in the homily, and psalms are sung; the prayers, collects, and liturgical songs are scriptural in their inspiration, and it is from Scripture that actions and signs derive their meaning. Thus, if restoration, progress, and adaptation of the sacred liturgy are to be achieved, it is necessary to promote that warm

and living love for Scripture to which the venerable tradition of both Eastern and Western rites gives testimony (art. 24).

Notice carefully how both preservation and transformation are necessary. For renewal, we go back to our tradition and find there eternal treasures. The centrality of the Scriptures has been a hallmark in the Christian tradition. Christians on all fronts are captivated with the Scriptures in these decades. A tremendously strong and pervasive biblical movement sweeps across the Christian world as we recover this central source of our faith, and Roman Catholics and Lutherans together share in this.

Catholics on the whole have also recovered the central importance of the homily as a prime vehicle for God's word, as the interpretation and application of the Scriptures. The general condition of Roman Catholic homilies remains far from ideal today; some commentators suggest that poor homilies are the single most divisive element in the church. At any rate, the laity are making ever greater demands on their clergy for well developed homilies that meet their needs and satisfy their hunger for a clear expression of God's word. This demand, with confident hope, must continue.

There are numerous areas of Roman Catholic/Lutheran convergence as regards eucharist and liturgy; it is indeed a happy and hopeful convergence. For, as Vatican II states, "...the liturgy is the summit toward which the activity of the church is directed; at the same time, it is the fountain from which all her power flows" (art.10).

Toward the Future   As we look to the future, what practical steps might begin to take place in the effort toward unity? One possibility is that Lutherans and Catholics could exist together in some form of institutional unity. Today, you see a neighbor down the street and say "She is a Lutheran." Imagine the step toward unity in the human family that would be made if your first reaction to her was that she is of your faith, sharing the same name. An afterthought would be that she expresses that common faith vis-a-vis a particular historical tradition rooted in Luther, a tradition that complements your own distinct tradition.

The principle of unity amid diversity suggests that there need not be complete doctrinal agreement in order for such unity to take place. There would, of course, have to be agreement on the "higher rungs" of the "hierarchy of truths." But the Lutheran/Roman Catholic dialogue suggests that such agreement already exists. Lutherans could acknowledge that papal leadership has a crucial place in the church to serve the unity of Christians and eventual human unity, though they would have a somewhat different relationship to the pope than Roman Catholics. Each side would retain its traditions while still existing in a wider unity.

A model of such unity can be seen in the Lutheran Church itself. For decades, Lutheranism in America has been divided into three primary groups: the American Lutheran Church (ALC); the Lutheran Church in America; and the Lutheran Church, Missouri Synod. In 1982, a historic moment took place as the first two and a part of the third (Association of Evangelical Lutheran Churches, AELC) agreed on a target date of 1988 for merging together as one Lutheran Church. It will consist of 5.5 million members and will be the third largest Protestant denomination in the United States, after Southern Baptists and Methodists. Two interesting themes surfaced in the remarks made by Lutheran leaders regarding the union. 1) The membership in the churches had desired union for quite some time, and their desires, in part, motivated the leaders to work on prospects for reunion. Thus, we see the importance of ecumenism beginning within the hearts of individual Christians. 2) The merger was spurred by the problems of human need in the world. Christians must unite first, as a sign of unity to the world, as a leaven that hastens the unity of all people.

Also, in 1982 Lutheran and Anglicans made a historic step by allowing limited intercommunion of members of the two churches. While this is, of course, not full communion, it marks a new degree of trust and represents a sharing that breaks through historic disunity. Similar first moves could be made between Roman Catholics and Lutherans.

Unfortunately, many members on both sides still cringe at the mention of ecumenical union under the mistaken assumption that they would then have to "become Catholics" or "become Lutherans," giving up their cherished tradition. Such, of course, is not the case at all. Eventual reunion will not take the form of some homogenous melting pot within which all traditions lose their distinctiveness to the church that would evolve as the "winner."

An alternative concrete possibility on the road to unity is that a general council could be convened in which all Christians would participate. The Augsburg Confession had originally called for such a council in order to settle differences, but the Roman Catholic Church refused. Then at Trent, Lutherans did not participate in the formative stages. Of course, a tremendous amount of further work would have to take place before such a council could eventually occur. It would have to be preceded by numerous smaller gatherings, on many levels—gatherings which have already begun in various locales, among various parishes.

And of course, the most significant concrete possibility ahead of us will not take place in dialogues or books or conferences but within each of us. Interior conversion, marked by careful study, enhanced by genuinely open interaction, is of the essence. As the Decree on Ecumenism insists, "There can be no ecumenism worthy of the name without interior conversion" (art.7).

QUESTIONS
FOR REFLECTION AND DISCUSSION

1.   Why do you think institutions, such as the church, are in constant need of renewal?

2.   "If the church is guided by the Holy Spirit, then it can't really make mistakes in the first place, and the concept of renewal or reform within the church is almost heretical." Respond to this statement.

3.   In what sense was Lutheranism originally a reform movement within the Catholic Church? What are the chief areas of the church's life that Luther felt were in need of reform?

4.   Historically, why did Lutheranism not remain within the church? With today's ecumenical efforts, could it be said that we "have another chance" at what was handled poorly in the sixteenth century?

5.   Can you describe the basic theme of the Reformation? Think about it in terms of a person's relationship to God.

6.   What does it mean to be "justified" before God? Can you think of an example from interpersonal relationships in which you have been "justified" before your friend?

7.   What was the original purpose of the Augsburg Confession? Might both Catholics and Lutherans rediscover the original intention of the document and follow through on it today?

8.   Luther began by criticizing, not condemning, the papacy. Why did he later change his moderate stance?

9.   How might papal reforms contribute to both the Catholic and Lutheran tradition?

10.   Why is it so significant that both sides share the same creed?

11.   Why are certain parts of the creed so difficult to understand without a sense of its historical development?

12.   How did Christological problems contribute to the formation of our creed?

13.   Why is it important that our mode of expressing the unchanging truths of Christianity be flexible enough to change from age to age and from culture to culture?

CHAPTER SIX

Anglicanism
The
Episcopal
Church

Anglicanism is a term that covers about twenty autonomous churches around the world that are in communion with the See of Canterbury. In the United States, the branch of the Anglican church we are familiar with is the Episcopal Church whose members we call Episcopalians. The word "episcopal" derives from the Greek word for "overseer," and implies that the bishopric is the foundation of their governmental system. The Anglican communion is unified by the local bishops who claim a long line of historical succession reaching back to the early church.

We have all heard of the famous King Henry VIII and his many wives. He reigned from 1509 to 1547, during the heart of the Reformation on the continent. Henry married his late brother's widow, Catherine of Aragon, the daughter of the King of Spain. His primary motivation for the marriage was to strengthen diplomatic ties between England and Spain. However, Henry did not have a male child, heir to the throne, with Catherine.

There existed an understandable fear of political instability should Henry die without an heir since the house of Tudor—Henry's line—had only recently achieved the crown. Thus, Henry decided that it was best to put Catherine aside. He requested permission from the pope for an annulment on the basis that Catherine was his sister-in-law, making the marriage invalid in the first place. Interestingly, it had taken Henry twenty years to discover this impediment. The pope refused partly because it would have been quite unwise to offend Catherine by granting the annulment; Catherine was the aunt of emperor Charles V, with whom it was essential for the pope to remain on good terms.

Henry's reaction to the refusal was extreme. In the Supremacy Act of 1534, he had himself designated head of the Church of England and had all of the clergy reject the papacy. He married Anne Boleyn, already pregnant, and the marriage was sanctioned by the Archbishop of Canterbury, Thomas Cramer, and the English Parliament. Little did Henry know that his hopes would be shattered with the birth of a girl, Elizabeth, who would eventually take the throne herself.

It is important to note that Henry's actions did not in themselves cause the English Reformation. There was a myriad of other factors that had already laid the groundwork for an imminent upheaval. Henry's action was more the occasion for English Reformation, insofar as it was the first tipped domino, that sent the others falling. England was ripe for the upheaval, and we can point to at least three reasons for this.

Nationalism   The English had developed a strong sense of nationalism—a sense of national consciousness that exalts one nation above others. The idea of the pope's universal jurisdiction stood in sharp contrast to a nationalistic spirit, resulting in a longstanding resentment of the Catholic papacy, especially among the growing middle class. On a very concrete level, there was resentment over the money being taken out of England for papal fees and taxes. Thus, Henry's Supremacy Act was considered by many to be the ultimate fulfillment of their own opinions.

Against this nationalistic backdrop, a theory called Erastianism was in vogue. It was named after the sixteenth century Swiss physician Erastus, who did not actually hold the precise doctrine that came to bear his name. In a radical departure from the church/state relationship of the Holy Roman Empire, Erastianism held that the state was all-powerful over the church. Church structures and clergy were to uphold and reinforce the infallible government in power. This view is understandable insofar as it exists as a reaction to the previous tendency of the church to dictate state policy. Of course, both of these tendencies seem foreign to people who are used to the separation of church and state.

Anticlericalism   Another mood that permeated the English Church was a strong anticlericalism. This has its early roots in the teachings of Wycliffe in the fourteenth century who taught that each individual had immediate access to God and did not need a priest to mediate that relationship. In Henry's time, anticlericalism was especially directed toward the monasteries. Having impressive stature during the middle ages, they had declined spiritually by the sixteenth century and had become wealthy landowners. Thus, many in England saw the need for either reform or abolishment of monasteries.

What Henry in fact did serves as an example par excellence of how closely interconnected was the religious strand of a culture with the political/socio-economic strands. Henry closed the monasteries altogether and confiscated their property. The goods and property were subsequently sold to the rising middle class. So large was this transfer that it contributed substantially to a social and economic revolution. And this is but one isolated example of how the religious reforms of the sixteenth century both caused and were caused by the rise of the middle class out of poverty and medieval serfdom.

Readiness for Reform   Finally, the English were ready for the idea of Luther and other reformers from the continent. During the Renaissance, an enlightened spirit developed in England that questioned superstitious beliefs of the monks and lower clergy and led a general discontent and criticism of certain doctrines, such as transubstantiation. English scholars were in touch with the new ideas developing on the continent and they spread quickly to the English commonfolk. An example of this is the printing in English of the New Testament in 1526. William Tyndale had been to the continent to study with Luther, and so inspired, completed the popular translation.

A Protestant England did not occur instantaneously with Henry's Act of Supremacy, however. Henry himself resisted efforts to turn the Church of England into a reformed church, and so essentially the only change was a shift in power from pope to king. But with Henry's death in 1547, a new era of religious ferment really began, an era that Henry had but touched off. The English masses would oscillate from one extreme to another in the decades following Henry's death, as monarchs of differing religious persuasions took the throne.

The first successor was Edward VI, Henry's only son, from his third marriage which was with Jane Seymour. Protestant forces now gained control and Cranmer, Archbishop of Canterbury, directed liturgical reforms. Parliament imposed new articles of faith, and a new prayerbook, the Book of Common Prayer. But in 1553, the young and frail Edward died. Despite efforts for a Protestant king, Mary, the daughter of Henry and Catherine, took the throne. A devoted and militant Catholic, she restored papal authority in England, placing the English hierarchy in communion with Rome and restored the Catholic Mass. The thoroughly Protestant Cranmer was executed along with close to three hundred Protestants from the lower classes (these persecutions earned her the title "Bloody Mary"). This was not only an internal state of affairs; it reached international proportions when Mary announced her plans to marry Phillip II of Spain, whose whole reign was devoted to the restoration of Catholicism.

But Mary died after a short reign in 1558. Henry's daughter Elizabeth, from his marriage to Anne Boleyn, succeeded Mary. Since she was Protestant, this represented still another change in religion for the English people. This time the road was well paved: Mary's persecutions had alienated masses of people who until then had clung to the "old religion." The Anglican Church was established for good under Elizabeth though the transition was by no means smooth. She was opposed on several fronts.

Elizabeth did not originally want to suppress or persecute Catholics; she wished to steer a more moderate course. But the pope excommunicated her and, moreover, declared that her subjects were not morally bound to obey her. Such a papal attitude was considered subversive to the highly nationalistic English state. Thus, her suppression of Catholics (for example, she drove the Jesuits out of England) was primarily political rather than religious.

Additional anti-English sentiment came from Spain. They reversed the short-lived diplomatic and religious ties occasioned by the marriage of Mary and Phillip. Elizabeth caused even more resentment abroad—in Catholic countries—when she supported French Protestants financially and gave Protestants in Holland military support. Such actions led Phillip to send the famous Spanish Armada against England in 1588, which was badly defeated.

The Thirty-Nine Articles   Elizabeth consolidated the official Anglican doctrine when she issued the Thirty-Nine Articles in 1563, which were a revision of the articles of faith issued under Edward. These are discussed in detail below. There existed a number of Protestants who remained dissatisfied with the Articles, convinced that they retained too many Catholic/papist tendencies regarding belief, ritual, and government. Because they wanted to purify Anglicanism of these tendencies, they were called Puritans or Separatists. They tended to form a non-sacramental and non-liturgical church with a more democratic structure. As established Anglicanism gained more and more power during the reigns of James I (1603-1625), and Charles I (1625-1649), these Separatists began heading toward America where they could find more freedom to practice their views.

The Thirty-Nine Articles issued during Elizabeth's reign still stand today as the central doctrinal expression of the Anglican communion. Following is a summary of the main tenets. Note the influence of the reformers on the continent.

Any trace of seeing the Mass as sacrifice was abandoned. This, as we have already seen, was a reaction against the idea that the Mass was an action performed by man to obtain grace. God's grace was free and gratuitous and could not be earned by outward works. To symbolize this shift, stone altars that connoted the idea of sacrifice were replaced with wooden tables.

The use of Latin was abandoned in favor of the vernacular.

Auricular confession was abandoned. Here we can see the reaction against the priest as a necessary agent mediating a relationship with God.

A clear, symbolic break with Catholicism came with the abandoning of clerical celibacy. Cranmer, like Luther and Zwingli, took a wife. This, together with the previous point, reveals the shift away from clericalism.

Both the bread and wine were to be given to the laity at the communion service. This was a symbolic issue insofar as it put everyone on "equal footing" in their relationship to God. Again, there was no room for clericalism.

In regard to the real presence, a middle ground was sought between the Catholic doctrine of transubstantiation and Zwingli's stance.

New rites of ordination were introduced. It is interesting to note that the Catholic rite had included handing the priest the chalice and the bread; in the new rite he is handed only the Bible (recall the emphasis on *sola scriptura*).

Allegiance to the pope, as we have already seen, was clearly rejected. Nonetheless, a modified form of Catholic hierarchy was retained with bishops and archbishops. This emphasis on the historic episcopate is one of the most important features of Anglicanism. The idea of the priesthood of all believers, while certainly having an intrinsic value, could possibly have led to anarchy—each person his/her own ruler. So the Articles were careful to steer clear of any such tendency by affirming the episcopal structure for governing the Anglican Church.

The Spirit of Anglicanism   The concept of unity amid diversity describes very adequately the Anglican communion itself. Since 1867, a symbol of Anglican unity and diversity has been the annual Lambeth Conference of Bishops. These are unlike any official council or synod in that their conclusions are more suggestions than mandates. The bishops from around the world gather to express their minds and they arrive at certain conclusions and recommendations, but these are not binding on the local churches unless those churches so choose in their own councils.

In the report from the 1948 Lambeth Conference, the spirit of the Anglican communion was well described:

> (It is) a river that is made up of streams, each of which passes through a different country, each with a color drawn from the soil through which it passes, each giving its best to the full strength of the river, flowing toward that ocean symbolic of a larger comity when the Anglican communion itself will once again become part of a reunited Christendom. No one stream is superior to another. The glory of each is its contribution to this river which, while being enriched by all, enriches all the countries of the world wheresoever it flows (Quoted in Piepkorn II:174).

The inherent sense of pluralism in the Anglican communion allows it an original and creative balance of beliefs and doctrine. For example, it has no infallible teaching structure, but at the same time, it is not anarchistic. There is a definite sense of authority in the historic episcopacy, and the conclusions from the Lambeth Conference are taken with genuine seriousness. The church in each country has a synodal structure for arriving at binding decisions.

As stated above, Anglicanism originated as a comprehensive religion, which results in there being no one distinguishing doctrine. Its comprehensiveness includes a broad range from what is called high Anglicanism to low Anglicanism. This broad sweep contains valid elements from both Catholic thought and Reformation thought. The high church members can, in fact, be referred to as Anglo-Catholics, while the low church members tend to be Evangelicals. The Anglo-Catholics are, of course, very akin to ourselves. Roman Catholics would find much Anglo-Catholic liturgy and piety consonant with their own. The Evangelican strain tends toward less structure, with an emphasis on the individual's psychological relationship with God.

It is crucial to qualify carefully the above generalizations, however, from the perspective that even without Catholicism there exists a real pluralism of attitude and belief, a pluralism that has existed throughout history.

It can be somewhat misleading to claim a certain convergence between High Church Anglicans and Roman Catholics. Certainly that convergence exists when it comes to the official form of Roman Catholicism as handed down by the magisterium—what we might call a "high" Roman Catholicism. But the richness of Catholicism is not exhausted by that one form. The Anglican/Roman Catholic dialogue has cogently pointed this out:

> The experience of dialogue, inspired by a desire to be honest and to search for the truth, compels Roman Catholics to realize very quickly that there are to be found within their own fold as well the same lines of division which in the Anglican tradition constitute officially accepted movements. The Roman Catholic block has no longer—if it ever had—the monolithic character which spontaneously comes to mind. Hence the debating of questions leads often to a confrontation not of the two churches so much as of two ways of reading the data of the faith or of two ecclesial mentalities present in both groups. The Roman Catholic may on a particular point feel more at home with an evangelical position, for example, than with another, and vice-versa. The polyvalence of comprehensiveness thus obliges the Roman Catholic side on the one hand to become more open to a healthy pluralism, admitting that such does not necessarily destroy the unity of the faith and life, and, on the other hand obliges it to recognize...that diversity does exist in its own camp.... (ARC-Doc II: 39-40).

Is this in essence saying that Catholics and Anglicans are essentially the same? If so, then is the fear some have that as we move into the ecumenical arena, we will lose our precious identity a valid fear? Are we not falling into the trap of saying, "We're all really the same," the very trap that genuine ecumenism ought not fall into? To allay this fear, the following should be considered.

To begin with, Anglicanism contains an inherent latitude of belief and practice, that is, a latitude that is structured within the Anglican communion. As a communion of local churches, one could say that diversity is officially condoned by virtue of the fact that there are no absolute mandates coming from an official teaching office. Thus, latitude is built in. Critics will suggest that Anglicanism ends up without any identity, without any essence, but they misread the true spirit of Anglicanism. First, the local churches certainly do have their own distinctive identities. But second, and most importantly, if Anglicanism as a whole did not have an inherent diversity, it could scarcely justify its existence as an independent communion—its local churches would simply graft on to other communions, be they Catholic or Reformed. The very virtue of Anglicanism is that its diverse local churches are in fact united under a common historic episcopate.

Catholicism does not contain an inherent latitude of belief and practice, such is not its own virtue. Our church does have an official teaching office. While the vast majority of official pronouncements are not endowed with infallibility, nonetheless, each local congregation, if it is to call itself Catholic, is bound to take them with utmost seriousness. Each bishop is obligated to teach and endorse in his local church the teachings found, for example, in the encyclical letters. Where, then, does Catholic diversity fit in? First, the encyclicals themselves often allow and encourage diversity. While basic principles must be assented to, usually those can and ought to be assented to in diverse ways. And secondly, the encyclicals are not infallible. They are meant to address the values of the gospel to changing times and circumstances. Today's encyclical will contain a mandate different from one 50 years ago. It is inevitable that some laity, theologians, or clergy will find that their conscience dictates that they act or believe contrary to official teaching; this is part of the dynamic that exists within a pilgrim church that must be open to change and renewal. But all in all, the authoritative proclamation exists as the Catholic ideal of belief and practice, and however it is taken, it must be taken seriously. Thus, a genuine cohesiveness is the virtue of Roman Catholicism.

The Anglo-Catholic Movement   It is interesting and informative to consider the historical roots of the closeness between High Church Anglicanism and the official form of Roman Catholicism. It is this closeness that prompted the following statement in the Decree on Ecumenism:

> As a result (of the Reformation), many communions, national or denominational, were separated from the Roman See. Among those in which some Catholic traditions and institutions continue to exist, the Anglican communion occupies a special place (art. 13).

In the early 1800s, the Church of England was in a quite sorry state. Its existence was threatened by the secularistic forces that were so strongly rooted in the Age of Enlightenment. Parish life lacked vitality, and the education of the clergy left much to be desired. Students and scholars at Oxford University saw the need for profound renewal. Thus began the Oxford Movement, also known as the Anglo-Catholic movement. Headed by John Henry Newman, the movement began publishing its views in the *Tracts for the Times* in 1833 and had a profound and permanent effect on the Anglican Church. Although "tractarianism," as it is also called, was strongly anti-papist, it essentially emphasized Catholic dimensions of Anglicanism in its quest for renewal. These dimensions included the importance of apostolic succession, a piety that saw grace mediated through the sacraments, a new interest in private confession, and a strongly ascetic spirituality. Another interest that developed more gradually was a strong emphasis on ritual. The utlimate result of the Oxford Movement was to retrieve a permanent Catholic dimension for the Church of England.

In 1841, a fascinating development began to take place in the life of John Henry Newman. He published Tract 90, in which he attempted to demonstrate that the Thirty-Nine Articles were, in fact, quite consonant with Roman Catholicism from a doctrinal standpoint. In a more ecumenical age, this might have been acceptable, but as it turned out, Newman was censured by the University as well as by a number of Anglican bishops. For several years he led a disciplined life of prayer and study, and during this time, he carefully examined the works of the early church fathers. He came to believe that the most authentic tradition coming down from the early church and the fathers was, in fact, the Roman Catholic tradition, and in 1845, he left the Anglican Church. He was ordained a Catholic priest and eventually became a cardinal. A number of his friends followed suit.

A number of Newman's ideas, alongside his life itself, are of great import to modern ecumenical theology. One example is his concept of tradition. Newman sheds a healthy light on tensions created by varying views about the value and role of tradition showing how tradition is not something fixed, but rather something that is necessarily fluid and in movement. There are for Newman two kinds of tradition: episcopal and prophetical. Episcopal tradition is the definitive and explicit framework of beliefs that is handed down from bishop to bishop throughout the ages—thus, the importance of apostolic succession. It is a tangible set of doctrines that is written down. There is certainly a fixed dimension to this sense of tradition.

But tradition is more than this. There is also what Newman called prophetical tradition, which cannot be neatly contained in a document and cannot be adequately expressed in statements. We have said before that our formulations of the truth we have received always fall short of the fullness of that truth. Prophetical tradition is precisely that—the fullness and richness of our vital and living tradition that escape neat formulation. It may be written down, but the writing will never fully express it. It is the on-going life of the church as it journeys through different times and cultures. As such, tradition is necessarily developmental in character. This is essential to realize as we move closer and closer ecumenically with other Christians. All of our various traditions are developmental, and it is our task to guide the development of our traditions closer together.

The Place of the Eucharist   During the Middle Ages there was a tendency to see the eucharist as an action done by the priest rather than as something done by the whole community. In essence, the priest was offering a sacrifice (performing a work) which people must attend (again, a work) in order to remain on good terms with God. The reformers reacted against this with the belief that God's gifts to humanity were totally gratuitous, completely free, rather than earned. Christ had offered the perfect sacrifice, once and for all, and no work on humanity's part could add to that. It could not be redone or re-performed just as we pleased—Christ was not at the priest's beck and call. The Anglicans, like other Reformation Churches, firmly rejected the concept of "Mass Sacrifices" in the Thirty-Nine Articles.

In 1971, the Anglican/Roman Catholic dialogue developed an "Agreed Statement on the Eucharist" in which they came to terms with the idea of the Mass as sacrifice. A healthy middle course was steered between two extremes. On the one hand was the extreme position that the reformers reacted against, the idea that the Mass is a sacrificial act we do to please, or appease, God. On the other hand is the other extreme that some of the reformers fell into, that of seeing the eucharist as a mere remembrance or memorial of the once and for all sacrifice without any transformative power ("lacking inherent efficacy" is the technical terminology).

In the dialogue, the participants worked out the problem by recovering the original Hebrew meaning behind the Passover meal. The Christian eucharist is a continuation—with a new content—of the Hebrew Passover feast. The Passover made present the mighty works of God, specifically the Exodus event. It was not merely a commemoration in which those works were recalled in the people's imaginations, but rather it was an event in which God's works were truly and efficaciously present to recreate the people. At the time of Christ, this was precisely how the Passover celebration was understood. And so when Christ instituted the eucharist, saying "Do this in memory of me," he did not mean that we were to repeat in any way his once-and-for-all sacrifice, nor did he mean that we should simply recall his sacrifice. He meant that in the eucharist something would happen, the event of salvation would be effected or made present again. This is precisely what is implied in the word "memorial," which in the Greek is *anamnesis* (Luke 22:19). As the dialogue states:

> ...the traditional understanding of sacramental reality, in which
> the once-for-all event of salvation becomes effective in the
> present through the action of the Holy Spirit, is well expressed
> by the word *anamnesis*. We accept this use of the word which
> seems to do full justice to the semitic background. Furthermore,
> it enables us to affirm a strong conviction of sacramental realism
> and to reject mere symbolism (Final Report, p.19).

In this new light, both extremes are avoided. First, the
eucharist is not a human act by which we affect or influence
God. "There can be no repetition or addition to what was then
accomplished once for all" (Final Report, p.13). And second,
it is not as if nothing real happens to us as we partake in the
eucharistic meal.

During the time of the Reformation, a great deal of super-
stition and "magic" had crept into Catholic piety regarding the
bread and wine of the eucharistic meal. The reformers reacted
in various ways to the Catholic doctrine of transubstantiation
(recall the controversy between Luther and Zwingli). Basically,
the Anglican Thirty-Nine Articles was to bring stability to a
very chaotic situation in which there were many extreme views
in competition with each other. The Anglican Church was hesitant to set forth, therefore, any one elaborate explanation of
how the change takes place in the eucharistic bread and wine.

In the recent Anglican/Roman Catholic dialogues, there
remains the same hesitancy to focus on any one elaborate explanation of the mystery of the eucharist. The agreed belief
in the real presence, opposing the Zwinglian source, is simply
stated: "Communion with Christ in the eucharist presupposes
his true presence, effectively signified by the bread and wine,
which in this mystery, become his body and blood" (Final
Report, p.14). Notice the important use of the word "mystery,"
and also the use of the word "effectively," which reinforces
the point we made earlier that there is a real effect in the
eucharistic celebration. It is not just a commemoration, but
an event in which Christ is present in his redeeming death and
resurrection.

Amid the somewhat technical details of this eucharistic
discussion, there is a very practical as well as painful issue at
hand. Can Catholics and Anglicans share communion together?

When you attend an Anglican liturgy, you may be impressed by how similar it is to a Roman Catholic liturgy. And at the communion service, you might think to yourself, "What better way is there of showing my willingness to be united than to share in the eucharistic meal together with these fellow Christians?" There is one theological tendency that would encourage such intercommunion even though we remain separated. According to this tendency, ecumenism begins at the grassroots level, and people can and must express their desire for unity and their real feelings of unity by sharing in the meal together. Such sharing will help push ecumenical efforts toward full reunion by institutionalizing unity, in one way, among communicants.

However, there is a second theological tendency, more prominent in Roman Catholicism that emphasizes the need to admit honestly that we do remain separated. The good will expressed in prematurely sharing the meal together is just that—premature. We are not united, and so it is dishonest to engage in an expression of unity.

The two stances are obviously in tension with one another. One might argue with the official Catholic stance that it keeps us from doing something concrete in working toward reunion in our own small ways. However, it might be good to consider the pain felt at not sharing eucharist as something very concrete in itself, something that will truly motivate us to hasten our movement toward unity. Consider what the dialogue has to say:

> In the concrete ecumenical situation...we suffer a nagging temptation to rush to institutionalize the degree of agreement we have undoubtedly reached....The problem arises when, without care, we urge...a degree of sacramental sharing which is not supported by this degree of agreement. It is one thing to ask for greater eucharistic hospitality; it is another to request general intercommunion. A Roman Catholic cannot accept the latter request because he finds therein a basic ambiguity.... receiving our holy communion we attest not only our belief in the presence, in sacrament, of the Body and Blood of the risen Lord, but also in the unity of the church. If that unity is not yet given, then we are better servants if we accept the pain of our

division....our way to unity is not only a great grace but...it is also the way of the cross (ARC-DOC III: 68-69).

Ministry, Priesthood, and the Historic Episcopate   You may recall that many abuses existed on the part of the Catholic hierarchy at the dawn of the Reformation. Luther reacted strongly against the exclusivism that was exhibited by much of the Catholic clergy. Monastic vows, for example, were thought to put the monk or nun into a "higher class" of Christians. Such an idea was especially ludicrous in light of the abuses existing within various orders. Much of this "higher class" had abandoned celibacy and lived more like kings and queens than like humble witnesses to the gospel and servants of others. In reaction to this, Luther stressed that Christ is our high priest and that there is a priesthood of all believers.

The Catholic practice of "many Masses—for those who could buy them—tended to neglect the once-and-for-all sacrifice of Christ. So too, the clergy as mediators between man and God, in their sorry state, neglected the one mediator, Christ, who alone had the power to justify us. As the Letter to the Hebrews states:

> ...we have been sanctified through the offering of the body of Jesus Christ once for all. Every other priest stands ministering day by day, and offering again and again those same sacrifices which can never take away sins. But Jesus offered one sacrifice for sins and took his seat forever at the right hand of God....By one offering he had forever perfected those who are being sanctified (10:10-14).

Thus, we can say that the primary priesthood of the New Testament belongs to Christ alone.

Along these same lines, Luther emphasized that every person who is baptized receives equal forgiveness from Christ, the true high priest, and is equally justified or accepted. The human act of belonging to some special class did nothing extra to merit salvation, since nothing we do can in and of itself helps in that regard. Thus we find the term "priesthood of all believers" expressing the reformers' ideas. We could call this a second priesthood, under the first priesthood of Christ.

One of the key words used in the documents of Vatican II to define the church is "the people of God." This represented a tremendous shift of emphasis. The church was not first and foremost a hierarchial structure that common people latched on to—though the hierarchy is profoundly important. Rather, the people themselves constitute the church, with the hierarchy existing to serve the church (recall the principle of subsidiarity). With this new understanding, Catholics and the churches of the Reformation find themselves closer than ever before in regard to ministry. Anyone who is baptized is commissioned to minister before God. We are all part of the church; we all share in a common priesthood.

Among the whole people who are the church, all communions also recognize the human need for leadership or for specific ministries amid the broader ministry that everyone shares. This could be called a third form of priesthood. Since the Reformation, a variety of ministerial forms emerged. These ranged from the extremely democratic Congregational structure, to a Presbyterian structure governed by elders in partnerships, to an Episcopal structure governed by individual bishops . A great deal of disagreement has occurred throughout the centuries as to which form of ministry is the most authentic. Happily, Lutherans, Orthodox, and Catholics are all in agreement on the importance of an episcopal structure government and the ordination of ministers by bishops. Despite this agreement, however, we do not all recognize each other's ministries as valid.

This problem stems back to the time of the Reformation. Luther and the reformers wanted to be part of the Roman Catholic Church and wanted Catholic bishops to continue ordaining ministers for them. This unity never materialized and Catholic bishops refused to ordain priests who belonged to the Reformation. Lutherans ended up having their priests ordain other priests. At the Council of Trent, all ordinations in the Lutheran Church were declared invalid.

The reason for this has to do with the concept of "apostolic succession." In our creed, we state that our church is "one, holy, catholic, and apostolic." Being apostolic means being true and faithful to the teachings of the original apostles. There are traditionally two ways of being faithfully apostolic. One way is through a succession of doctrine. According to this mode, one is apostolic if one's teaching of the faith is authentically in line with that of the original apostles. This approach, however, has numerous difficulties. Someone could claim apostolic teaching while in reality that teaching would be quite heretical. This happened more and more often as the church adapted itself to ever new and changing situations (recall for example, some of the early Christological heresies).

As a result of this problem, a second mode of apostolic succession was increasingly employed. Doctrinal authenticity was made the special responsiblity of certain individuals— bishops—in succession to one another starting with the original apostles. Only bishops within this unbroken line could validly ordain priests. If someone individually decided to take authority and ordain ministers, their priesthood would be considered invalid within Roman Catholicism. There is a presupposition here that at ordination the priest is changed and receives a "stamp" or character that forever confers the power and authority to perform sacramental acts that others cannot validly perform. If the priest is not ordained by a bishop in the line of succession, the ordination is invalid, and the character is missing. This view is exemplified in the Roman Catholic tradition that not just anyone can say Mass, consecrate the bread and wine, forgive sins, or baptize. And likewise, not just anyone can ordain a priest, endowing him with the sacramental character. It can only be done by a bishop in the proper line of succession.

In this light, one can see why Roman Catholicism has refused to recognize the validity of Lutheran ministry, since at the time of the Reformation ordination was considered to have taken place in an improper mode. This also sheds light on another reason why Catholics have not been allowed to receive communion at services outside their own church. If other ministers are considered "invalid," then technically, they cannot truly consecrate the bread and wine. Sound ecumenical theology, of course, moves away from such a position, as we shall see shortly.

Anglicans see the importance of apostolic succession of individual bishops, as well as the impact of this on the validity of their ordinations. The episcopal structure is essential for them, so much so that the Lambeth Conference of 1888 declared the historic episcopate a prerequisite for any discussion of a reunited Christendom. And, of course, Anglicans see in their own church structure a true and definite line of succession back to the apostolic church. It is, therefore, with great frustration and consternation that they hear the Roman Catholic pronouncement that their succession is not true and their ordinations are invalid.

When Elizabeth I took the throne and reestablished the reformed religion once again, it was necessary to replace the Roman Catholic bishops from Mary's reign with ones who were Anglicans. Elizabeth reinstated four who had originally been Anglican bishops under Edward VI. Two of these four men had been ordained in the time of Henry VIII when Catholic episcopal structure was intact, and so their validity is unquestionable. But the other two had been ordained in the reformed religion under Edward and, therefore, are not recognized by Catholics as valid bishops—they were outside the line of succession. In 1559, these four men consecrated the new (and first Elizabethan) Archbishop of Canterbury, Matthew Parker. The next generation of priests and bishops were ordained through Parker, and so if his orders are considered valid, theirs are valid also, as well as all succeeding Anglican priests.

But there is an even deeper and more fundamental reason why Anglican orders could be considered invalid that lies at the foundation of the first reason just outlined. The very rite of ordination itself that the Church of England used was considered defective from the Roman Catholic perspective. You may recall that the sacrament of ordination has a definitive effect, called the "character," on the person ordained. With this character is bestowed the priestly power to consecrate the elements and offer authentically the true sacrifice of the eucharist. This character is called the inward effect of the sacrament of ordination, that is, a real change takes place. However, a sacrament must also signify in an outward way that which it causes or effects in an inward way. This "outward signification" consists of two things according to traditional Roman

Catholic sacramental theology: matter and form. The matter is the actual laying on of hands, bishop to priest in the ordination rite. The form is the spoken words. The two combine to signify outwardly that which is caused inwardly.

The words used in the Roman Catholic rite of ordination, then, would make explicit reference to that which was happening within the priest being ordained—namely, a definitive power being conferred. Reformed theology, however, reacted against certain elements associated with the Roman Catholic priesthood: the idea of the priest having power to change the elements (transubstantiation), the notion that the priest was offering a sacrifice, and the underlying concept that the priest, in fact, had an exclusive power and was necessary for mediating God to people. The new Anglican rite of ordination, therefore, contained no mention of these things. Thus, from a Roman Catholic perspective, the whole outward signification of the Anglican rite did not express or intend what ought to be happening inwardly during the rite. Not only was the outward signification considered defective, but the whole Anglican intention behind the rite was also considered defective. Thus, all Anglican orders would be considered invalid.

Working toward a Solution   In the late 1800 s, fresh interest arose in regard to the validity of Anglican orders. Scholars and churchmen on both sides felt that the Catholic position could be reexamined. Careful scrutiny of the whole situation took place, but the result was negative. In 1896, in the bull *Apostolicae Curae,* Pope Leo XIII declared all Anglican orders to be null and void. This remains the official—though not infallible—Roman Catholic position.

Leo presupposed that there was but one avenue by which ordinations could be considered valid, namely, for all priests to be "properly" ordained by bishops who trace their succession back to the apostolic church. However, this presupposition can be questioned today for several reasons.

There is a silence in the New Testament concerning a cultic priesthood. Jesus himself never clearly spelled out either the specific duties of priests or a specific rite of ordination. Furthermore, historically there exists a gap between the apostles and what later emerged as a bishopric that claimed to be in direct succession to them. Individual apostolic succession was probably not at all a concern of the first apostles. For Roman Catholics, it is tradition that provided the means of succession and the official rite of ordination. The reformers, on the other hand, denied tradition as a source of revelation and turned to Scripture alone (*sola scriptura*). Thus, it is not surprising that they departed from both the Roman Catholic rite of ordination and the whole belief that Orders was actually a sacrament, since neither of these appear explicitly in the Scriptures.

A focus on this second mode of succession suggests that asking whether Anglican orders are valid historically is to begin with the wrong question. The better question to start with is whether we can agree on the nature of ministry. The Anglican/Roman Catholic dialogue suggests that there is such agreement. We both agree that the ministry is essential for leadership in the church. We agree that the minister must be a faithful witness to the gospel, must be officially ordained, and that the ordination is permanent. It is in this new context that we can move on to recognize the validity of one another's ministry.

Starting from such a new perspective and context, then, it would be necessary for the decision of *Apostolicae Curae* to be reversed. This is certainly possible, since we are in a new historical situation that makes new demands on Christians. For example, today we are in close agreement on the nature of the eucharist. At the time of the Reformation there was sharp disagreement, and that is essentially what led to a change on the Anglican side in the ordination rite. If we agree on eucharist today, then recognition of each other's ministries is the natural next step. This is part of the "new context" within which, according to the Final Report, we must consider validity of Anglican ordinations:

> ...our agreement on the essentials of eucharistic faith with regard to the sacramental dimension of the eucharist, and on the nature and purpose of priesthood, ordination, and apostolic succession, is the new context in which the questions should now be discussed. This calls for a reappraisal of the verdict on Anglican Orders in *Apostolicae Curae* (p.45).

Thus, we find a classic example of a) going back in history, to discover the source of a disagreement, b) realizing that in our new historical situation that source for disagreement no longer exists (step four), and therefore, c) accepting joyfully that we are closer to one another than we had thought, and d) forgiving one another for the polemically charged disagreements of the past.

It is most fitting to conclude our journey into the Anglican communion with a concrete example of an ecumenical relationship. In 1971, parishioners of an Anglican and Roman Catholic parish entered into a covenant relationship with one another. In a sermon on the new relationship is found a prime example of the two key themes of unity—the two parishes united, recognizing each other's validity, and identity—they each continue to retain their distinctive traditions. In other words, unity amid diversity.

> After more than 400 years of isolation and alienation, our two communions are declaring our friendship for each other. When you look down the road and see what this step we are about to take signifies, who can fail to be exhilarated by the warmth of the reconciliation we now have?.... The joy we have can be compared to that which we have when the cure to a dread disease has been discovered. Our division has been very much like a disease which has sapped the strength of Christ's church. Now happily a cure has been found.

Intercommunion does not mean one church will absorb the other or that we will both be absorbed in a bigger church. We are not aiming at a new political structure with a new constitution. Each communion—Anglican and Roman—will retain its own identity, character, ethos, and distinctive qualities. To use colloquial idioms, we will continue doing our own thing, dancing in our own style, but dancing as partners to the same tune (Quoted in Arc-Doc III: 42-43).

QUESTIONS
FOR REFLECTION AND DISCUSSION

1. What are some commonly held myths about the origins of the Episcopal Church?

2. What is your initial reaction to the historical circumstances that sparked the separation between England and Rome?

3. How did political concern dominate the chain of events?

4. What are some examples of pluralism within Roman Catholicism?

5. How are Anglican comprehensiveness (diversity) and Roman Catholic cohesiveness (unity) each important?

6. Using Newman's insights, respond to the viewpoint that tradition (or doctrine) is static and unchanging.

7. How is Newman's thought important to Roman Catholicism and to ecumenism?

8. How does the principle that "agreement comes about by reaching back through history to our common origins" apply to the current Anglican/Roman Catholic understanding of eucharist as sacrifice?

9. How has dialogue on this issue clarified or expanded your own understanding of eucharist?

10. How can the pain of not sharing eucharist be a motivating factor toward unity?

11. How can the notion of an ordained priesthood be reconciled with the notion of a common priesthood shared by all baptized persons?

12.   How did historical events affect the issue of valid ordinations?

13.   How have you generally understood "apostolic succession"? What else can this term mean?

14.   What is the importance of resolving the problem of the validity of orders?

15.   Why is it important that the Roman Catholic position on Anglican orders is not an infallible one?

16.   How has your study of Anglicanism helped you to better understand that church? Has it enhanced your understanding of Roman Catholicism?

CHAPTER SEVEN

The Presbyterian Reformed Tradition

The Presbyterian Church takes its name from a representative form of church government. The Greek word *presbyteros* means "elder," and Presbyterians are governed by ordained teaching elders and elected ruling elders. Local congregations are supervised by presbyteries, or associations of the larger church, which govern in various geographical areas.

If Presbyterians were asked to name themselves according to their theology or beliefs, rather than their form of government, they would probably choose "Reformed," in the tradition of John Calvin, the French/Swiss reformer who lived one generation after Luther. Although Presbyterians are not Calvinist in their belief, they still would trace their theological roots back to Calvin.

In the last chapters, we have carefully noted how good ecumenism has a certain element of paradox in it, in that various Christian communions need to open themselves outwardly to the riches of other traditions while at the same time becoming more conscious of and committed to the riches of their own tradition (step two). A spokesman for the Presbyterian Church summed up this crucial attitude rather compellingly:

> There are Presbyterians today...in whose spirit something paradoxical is taking place. On the other hand, we can say, unequivocally and unashamedly, "We never felt ourselves to be more Presbyterian than we do today." But then we go on to add, "We never felt ourselves to be less Presbyterian than we do today." Both affirmations are true. We are less Presbyterian than ever before because we never, for a moment, allow ourselves to believe that Presbyterianism exhausts the Christian religion...on the other hand, we were never more Presbyterian today because we believe that there are insights in our Presbyterian heritage of faith, and attitudes in our Presbyterian tradition of life, which the Church Universal needs in this tremendous hour (John Mackay, quoted in Piepkorn II:275).

Often we assume that if someone is seriously looking into other "belief systems" or perspectives, then that person is somewhat insecure about his or her own identity and looking for something new to graft on to. Catholic ecumenism carries with it no such insecurity. We are fully secure within the riches of our own tradition. But because we know that no one can exhaust the fullness of our gracious God, we can always allow ourselves to be enriched by other traditions. With this spirit, we begin our discovery of the Presbyterian tradition.

As we look to the origins of Presbyterianism, we all find ourselves even more deeply immersed in the age of the Reformation building upon the groundwork laid in the previous chapter. Looking back at this extraordinary age from our own twentieth century viewpoint, we are struck by the types of controversies that ensued, and even more so at the amazing amount of energy and vigor with which they were pursued. As we explore this age in more and more depth, to keep a proper perspective, several attitudes are in order.

Realize first that this was an age of unparalleled religious earnestness. These issues at hand were not left in the pew on a Sunday morning, but rather formed in a vital way the day to day consciousness of common people. The main reason for this is quite complex, though also quite understandable in light of our present day situation. Many of the values and institutions—political, economic, religious—that had stood the test of time were toppling down. They were being dissolved in large part by that movement, of such magnitude that it escapes simple definition, called the Renaissance. Unimaginable violence, change, and uncertainty caused everyone to grope with almost insatiable desire for something permanent, something to provide at least some feeling of control. The issues discussed in these chapters were so vital to those people because they performed precisely that role.

Secondly, this search for something permanent was a search in the realm of mystery—that spiritual realm that cannot be seen by the eye as something tangible and empirical. It is transcendent, beyond material reality, and is seen with the eyes of faith. Our culture is largely biased against the transcendent, because it is unwilling to assent to that which cannot be proven by logical deduction and empirical observation. It is nonetheless quite real (or even, with the eyes of faith, more real), and the Christian holds that one's life is diminished by its absence. Thus, the perplexing controversies of the age of the Reformation can challenge us or invite us to take with utmost seriousness and earnestness the transcendent dimension— as much in our midst as for the people of the sixteenth century, or any age. Of course, we will be the better for pursuing this dimension with a more ecumenical spirit.

In this perspective, let us return to the Reformation era. Those things in the Catholic Church which had so deeply troubled Luther were given immediate attention by many others as well. Many longed for reform, wishing to return to the excellence of an earlier, more biblical faith from which people had strayed in the course of history. There were many who, like Luther initially, sought renewal within the boundaries of the established church. A well-known example is Thomas More who, though certainly aware of needed reform, was willing to go along with the radical change of King Henry VIII because of his sincere fidelity to the Catholic Church. Many such men were appalled at the final result of Luther's revolt and did their best to tame it. The Council of Trent, for example, can be seen in this light. On the other hand, however, there were many who felt Luther had not gone far enough and longed for a more thorough break from a Catholicism that, in their minds, had gone so completely awry that a clean break was necessary in order to retain true gospel values. Herein lies the birth of another Reform tradition besides the Lutheran one; its two most significant founders were Ulrich Zwingli and John Calvin.

Ulrich Zwingli   Appearing first was Zwingli, an ex-priest working to reform the Christian faith in Switzerland from his position as pastor of the main parish in the city of Zurich. Perhaps even more than Luther, Zwingli saw a gap between a powerful, transcendent God and finite man in the corrupted world of materiality. This god, for Zwingli, could not be approached by anything in our world of sense experience. Thus, the very concept of sacrament was foreign to Zwingli, it being an instance of God gracing human beings vis-a-vis a material sign in the created order. Like Luther, Zwingli reacted against all those "superstitious" practices within Catholicism that were so tied to the visible, material order (the realm of works); belief in saints and their images, incense and candles, indulgences, and, of course, that ultimate example of human pride, the priest consecrated as a special agent with miraculous powers elevating him above the common person.

Zwingli believed that nothing miraculous could occur on a simple communion table. In this, Luther and Zwingli seriously disagreed. You will recall how Luther believed in the real presence of Christ in the eucharist, a belief illuminated by the analogy of the iron in the fire. With this doctrine (called substantiation), Luther refused to completely eliminate the real presence of Christ's body and blood in the eucharist, that element so strongly upheld in the Catholic doctrine of transubstantiation. Zwingli took a full step beyond Luther, insisting that the eucharist was nothing more than a memorial service. It commemorated a past event and represented figuratively a present one, the coming of Christ in grace to the assembled Christians mindful of his suffering for them. But Christ was not in the bread and wine. The eucharist is not sharing sacramentally in the actually present mystery of the crucified Christ. The whole notion of sacrament was blasphemous, closing an irreducible gap between God and man, essentially idolatry. Keep in mind in all this the unpleasant associations and abuses that went with the notion of sacrament at the time. This disagreement between Luther and Zwingli led to the split between Lutheran Protestantism and Reformed Protestantism. One can think of Luther as taking a step to the left (using the political term) of Catholicism, and Zwingli taking still another step. The split involved condemning one another's doctrines and refusing to celebrate the Lord's Supper together. Zwingli got the civil governments of Zurich and Berne to support his type of reform, and it also later spread elsewhere in Switzerland and Southern Germany. But his movement by itself did not produce an organized church with Zwingli as founding father. He died before his movement was a decade old in a battle lost to the Swiss cantons that remained Catholic in 1531. Nonetheless, the groundwork was laid in Switzerland for Protestant domination spearheaded by still another charismatic reformer.

John Calvin   Calvin was originally from France, and his early years were in many ways like Luther's. Both their fathers were ambitious men who climbed high on the socio-economic ladder. Both of the young men were given superior educations. Perhaps most importantly, both experienced profound spiritual crises, which led eventually to a conversion experience. The difference in their conversions, however, is perhaps grounded in their distinctive temperaments. While Luther was outgoing and emotional, undergoing much torment on his spiritual journey, Calvin was more private and scholarly, and his conversion to Protestantism came gradually during his early twenties. He was stoic, austere, and morally rigorous, but he was not inhuman as many have made him out to be. He suffered an unbelievable array of physical ailments, which may account for his occasionally violent temper and also the stoic earnestness that lies behind his theology.

The young Calvin began a journey from Paris to Strasbourg in 1533. On his way, he went through Geneva and was influenced there by a leading reform preacher, William Farel, who threatened him with God's condemnation if he didn't remain. The city had renounced the rule of its prince-bishop and needed new governmental structures, including a new reformed church order. Calvin was needed for the reform, since he was a legal as well as theological scholar. He did, in fact, rewrite the city's administrative code and eventually became one of its main pastors. By 1537 he had prepared the Geneva Confession, a design for a thoroughly reformed and Christian city. However, when he tried to get all the citizens to sign the confession, there was so much hostility that both he and Farel were forced to leave. Confusion reigned in Geneva until he was invited back in 1541. By the 1550s he had transformed Geneva into a model Protestant city through the deployment of his presbyterial form of government, which related closely to the city government. A "Protestant Rome" had been created. People from all over Europe (from places where radical republican Protestantism was forbidden), flocked to Geneva, later to return to their native lands thoroughly immersed in Calvinistic ideals.

What are the hallmarks of Calvinistic theology which held such force for the people of the time? Calvin, like Luther, held that human beings were inclined to sin from birth and could only be justified by trusting in God's mercy. Looking around them, they viewed that God had actually gifted very few persons with the grace of justification. This view was in no little part a reaction against the optimism of the Catholic Church: if one arranged things properly—indulgences, sacraments, and other works—salvation was guaranteed. For Calvin, the choice of salvation was strictly God's. Any attempt to enlarge on the capacity of human beings for attaining salvation became, in Calvin's eyes, an attempt to shift the choice from God to people.

If this last phase is accepted as true, then there is but one logical conclusion to be drawn from it, a conclusion to which Calvin, like Luther and Augustine, had also been forced: God predestines whom God will elect and bring to salvation. Calvin, and with even greater emphasis some later Calvinists, went on to draw the implied corollary: God predestines all the others knowingly to damnation in hell.

One must admit that so far Calvin's logic—and a symmetrical and orderly thinker he was—appears flawless. His logic continues into discussion of Christ's death. If salvation is granted to people by Christ's atoning death, and if only the elect are predestined to be saved, then it is only consistent to claim that Christ died for the elect or predestined only, not all humanity. This is called the doctrine of limited atonement. Those who are luckily numbered among the elect cannot resist God's saving grace. The others are incapacitated, unable to respond to it positively. Of course, the bothersome thing in all this is that there is absolutely no room left for free choice in dealing with God. Calvin, though, remains consistent and contends that we are not free to respond or not respond to God's will in our regard.

At this point one becomes quite suspicious, quite aware that freedom is but one side of the coin, the other being responsibility. If we are not free, then we are also not responsible; and what could cause the breakdown of society more than an outright denial of responsibility? But Calvin's society did not break down, because Calvin simply turned around and held people responsible for their sins before God. Therein lies the one inconsistency in his thought, and it is no small inconsistency at that.

Yet the one thing that must be said for Calvin's thought was that it worked. Though theoretically inconsistent to anyone who sees freedom as an essential condition for responsibility, imagine the immense psychological power it could hold over a person. If you accept the basic tenets of the Calvinist system—that the elect are few, and that you are responsible— you are going to lead a life resembling as closely as possible your image of what a member of the elect's life would look like.

This intense psychological power contributed to the smooth workings of the Geneva commonwealth. Each week an appointed consistory passed judgment on all who had been accused of improper behavior. This is an example of the sometimes oppressive supervision of the life of community members. A certain austerity was built into daily life, with the conviction that many worldly pleasures did not lead one on the path to salvation and thus had to be severely curbed. The worship service concentrated on preaching of the word—including fear of hell to motivate moral behavior—and on weekly eucharist. On the issue of the real presence, Calvin took the position that Christ was really present in the eucharist, spiritually but not physically.

To many Catholics, including this writer, there is a certain uneasy reaction to Calvin's thought. Several nuances should be pointed out in order to keep it in perspective. As we mentioned earlier, this was an age of great religious earnestness, and the original Calvinist movement had a tremendous appeal for people of this time. As the original movement declined, though, a much more forbidding and puritanical image overshadowed the original spirit. Our tendency is to identify this darker image with the original movement. Also, the key themes in Calvin's thought are found throughout Christian thought. His original inspiration was Saint Augustine. More recently, in our own tradition, we find the Jansenists of the seventeenth century struggling with the same logic and striving for ever greater consistency.

Augustine and Luther, Calvin and the Jansenists focused great attention trying to state how God relates to his people and to what extent God wills the salvation of all people everywhere. It is actually more within our finite abilities to state that our salvation is a mystery—that key word that opens so many ecumenical doors, and likewise closes so many when not appreciated. It is not revealed to us whether a large or small portion of humanity is going to be saved. Instead, we have several mysteries in our midst. On the one hand, we know God is all-loving and desires salvation for everyone. On the other hand, God's distinctive gift to us—that which dignifies us and raises us about the animals—is freedom. We can misuse our freedom, putting our salvation in peril. It seems that if God is omnipotent, and if God is all-loving (desiring that we be saved), then God would cause everyone to be saved. God could do it and God would want to do it. The fact that God doesn't do this seems to indicate, on the surface, God's weakness. But this is all according to human logic. God's love,

God's power, they all coalesce as a great and unfathomable mystery. We are tempted to figure it out, and that is fine. But it is best to simply behold it in reverence. A key to good ecumenism is the realization that in the "figuring out" phase, there will invariably be diversity, which is fine and necessary. In the beholding phase, there can be genuine unity. The humility that this phase demands can draw us together.

We can conclude our historical sketch by considering the aftermath of Calvin's contribution. His influence was immense. Those who had been immersed in his system in Geneva took the Reformed Church model to many geographical areas: to Scotland, where it was promulgated by the great preacher and organizer John Knox; to England, from where it came to Plymouth in New England and even influenced the form of government in the United States; to the Low Countries, where it was instrumental in the Dutch revolt against the Spanish; it even spread to parts of Eastern Europe: Bohemia, Poland, and Hungary. Although they suffered persecution in many places, Calvinist Christians were often in the right place at the right time to achieve great wealth and political power: the Netherlands with its overseas commerce; the England of the Civil War and Oliver Cromwell, with its American and Irish colonies; the Prussia of Frederick the Great. Even when the presbyterial form of government was not adopted, Calvinist ideas were propagated by English-speaking Protestants all over the world. America's Pilgrims and Puritans fall under this larger heading, as do some Methodists and even Anglicans.

The situation in France, Calvin's original home, was quite different. There was strong historical precedent for reform of the church, as evidenced by the conciliar movement in the fourteenth and fifteenth centuries, which called the supreme authority of the pope into question. Calvin's ideas found ready acceptance among the French, though especially in the Southwest, where Protestant churches were organized. However, France was a centralized monarchy. Unlike the German princes who were only too happy to stir up trouble with Rome, King Francis I had signed a concordat that actually increased royal authority over the established Catholic Church—an even tighter welding of church and state. In this context,

Protestantism did not fight for toleration—it was simply inconceivable that citizens of the same political unit might practice different religious faiths. Rather, they had to fight to succeed Catholicism, and they lost after unimaginable bloodshed.

In this light, one can see the importance of understanding the history of those separated from us. Looking back in an historical context, we understand why various sides consolidated against one another in the decades and years following the initial Reformation. While the theological positions of the various sides certainly had validity, they had so long imputed bad faith to their opponents that bloody battles were inevitable. To our dismay, Presbyterians and Roman Catholics are still at it in Northern Ireland, a modern-day situation that gives us a hint of the religious-political battles of previous eras. With the benefit of hindsight, we can appreciate some of the reasons why we were originally separated, and then move forward in a more ecumenical spirit.

Presbyterians Today   Today, most Presbyterians have rethought Calvin's original ideas and have become more moderate; in fact, one may wonder whether Calvin would even recognize his modern-day followers. For example, they have taken part in the great twentieth century liturgical movement, which has touched all mainline churches. This is immensely significant for ecumenism insofar as it allows all Christians a common base; the recognition that our transcendent God can, in fact, be mediated through human and worldly things. The unbridgeable gap between us and God, as envisioned by Zwingli, Luther, and Calvin is now bridged. God remains transcendent, to be sure, but in art, in music, in symbolism—in a word, in sacrament—God can be found.

Presbyterians would also affirm free will today, moving beyond Calvin's original line of reasoning. The early opponent of predestination, in the late 1500s was Arminianism, spearheaded by the Dutch theologian, Jacob Arminius. He reacted against the harshness of predestination, convinced that election and damnation were not absolute in God's mind but conditional upon human choice. Also, Arminianism was more tolerant of worldly habits than the puritanical focus of Calvin. In these respects, modern-day Presbyterians have become much more Arminian.

During the past 15 years, Presbyterians and Roman Catholics have been involved in a long series of ecumenical discussions. While some of the discussions have been on a theological level, they have not proceeded in the same manner as the Lutheran/Catholic dialogue, for example. Instead, despite some criticism, the Roman Catholic/Presbyterian-reformed Consultation has embarked on a rather concrete and practical path, as reflected in its major public statement, *The Unity We Seek*. The primary question addressed by the consultation has been, "How can we obtain a balanced focus between the theological factors and the sociological factors?" In other words, the problem is how to look beyond ecumenical cooperation and "realistically envisage that unity which is the ultimate goal of ecumenism." The remaining parts of this chapter will reflect this practical orientation, following the organization of the official statement. We will discuss how we can find unity in our beliefs, structure, and worship.

Finding Unity in Belief

In step five of our ecumenical method (see Chapter One), we look to the basis upon which we can build our future unity, our common tradition. The Catholic/Presbyterian Consultation elucidates this step in an insightful way. Consider this statement of belief:

> As Christians, we all believe it has been divinely revealed that Jesus is God and Savior, sent by the Father to lead all creation under the guidance of the Spirit to salvation, to liberation, "to reconcile everything in his person" (Col 1:20). Our trust in Jesus assures us that God the Father has sent him, and still continues to work through him in the power of the Spirit (*The Unity We Seek*, p. 17).

In such a broad statement, two basic elements of our belief can be uncovered. On the one hand, there is the act by which we have faith in Jesus as our Savior, which is the act of trusting.

This can be termed our "faith-as-act" (also called faith-as-trust). On the other hand, we articulate that which we affirm in our trust, namely, that Jesus is God and Savior, sent to reconcile all things. This can be termed our "faith-as-content."

Our unity in belief must be founded on the first element, that act of trusting in something beyond us, something transcendent. This is at the heart of our tradition. When it comes to the second element, we also have much in common, namely, the fundamentals of our tradition. But this is also the area in which divergence occurs. Since the church is a living community, it expresses its faith-as-content in light of its on-going living experience. As it was handed down, the faith-as-content became more differentiated as it was applied in ever-new situations. Various traditions grew, developed, and diverged as they were handed down in a variety of contexts. In fact, the word "tradition" derives from a Latin word that means to pass on, as from hand to hand.

Though it need not be, this is the context of our disunity. Not all Christians agree when it comes to various refinements and applications of the faith-as-content. The mistake comes in not recognizing all along that the element of faith-as-trust did in fact remain the same, providing a common tradition— could it only have been seen. The Consultation articulates this well:

> When this lack of agreement reached sufficient intensity, the unity of the faith was rent; that is, in effect one group of Christians stated that another group's lack of affirming certain "essential" elements of the faith-as-content was so fundamental as to seem to imply that their trusting in God, their faith-as-act, was also essentially not Christian. But it is impossible for one group of Christians to assert with certitude that only they are in good faith, that is, have an authentic faith as act, as trust in God (p.18).

Yet the story of our past is the story of turning repeatedly to such assertions.

Approaching our disunity from this perspective is quite similar to what took place at the outset of the Lutheran/Catholic dialogue, as discussed in Chapter Five . The discussion started with our common creed, recognizing that we both share the same act of trust in God. When it comes to the faith-as-content, the precise articles of the creed, we also find mutual agreement. Multiplicity or plurality occurs as the two traditions journey through history on the level of faith-as-content while the level of faith-as-trust remains the same. Two moments in good ecumenism are taking place, the two moments described in step six of our ecumenical method. The common tradition is recognized, and the plurality in our traditions is recognized as essentially good.

What we have, then, is unity amid diversity. We can have a plurality of unique identities, a genuine diversity, and still be unified. The only reason that we lose our unity is that we convince ourselves that if we have differing views, we are therefore disunified. That does not have to be true. Everyone is unique, and life would be very boring and artificial if that were not so.

Thus, we can find a real unity in and through our diversity, for we all have a common goal and we can learn from one another on our pilgrimage toward that goal. In the final analysis, we are all searching for ultimate meaning in our lives, and we share the tradition that presupposes an ultimate meaning that comes only from trust in God and God's revelation in Jesus Christ. The meaning of life remains a mystery, and God remains a mystery. No matter how much we know, we never have the final answers arranged neatly in front of us. In our attempts to understand, we come up with a multiplicity of statements of faith (faith-as-content). But, since each statement ultimately comes from the same source and is oriented to the same goal (faith-as-trust), we can say that this multiplicity of statements is mutually complementary. None are complete; and if we put them all together, the statement would still be incomplete. Once we recognize this, we have broken a massive barrier and can sit down with one another and learn from one another. We can learn about one another's pasts, and the mistakes that have been made. We can learn about one another's present beliefs and allow those beliefs to broaden our minds and enrich our world views.

All of this involves a renewal of attitudes, or that key word, conversion. This is at the very heart of ecumenism; it is a groundwork that must be laid by individuals in local churches. It cannot be emphasized enough that this conversion toward a more open attitude is at the same time a conversion toward deeper commitment and loyalty to one's own tradition. Openness does not mean "anybody's idea is as good as anybody else's." Ideas can be mistaken. Or a good concept or belief can be taken to an extreme and misused. It is obvious that we have unique identities because we are convinced that our own particular formulation of belief, our own faith-as-content, is more accurate or more beneficial. But on the other hand, we cannot look down on someone else's belief, especially when our common denominator is the same, the mystery of Jesus Christ.

Finding Unity in Structure   All of this talk about unity and diversity must be translated on a practical, structural level. Very practical recommendations need to be made. The Catholic/Presbyterian Consultation made an effort to concretize this by suggesting that we need to enter into a period of transition toward unity in some very definite ways.

We said in step seven of our ecumenical method (Chapter One), that the ultimate goal was to be full communion. What does this mean? The world "catholic" means universal, and true catholicity means that we must work toward a "communion of communions," or a "church of churches." Notice that this concept, or model, for unity includes both the element of unity ("a communion") and the element of retaining our identities ("of communions"). There can be many communities gathered together in Christ, each retaining its own unique tradition. But we must be gathered together in Christ, and that means accepting one another, and accepting one another's differences. Unanimous consent on all issues will not be found, and even if it could, it would only make for boredom and artificiality. A real communion is lively and active because there are strong differences that do not destroy the unity.

What types of things can we do during this transitional period toward a communion of communions? Here we will mention seven approaches, taken from the conclusions of the Consultation.

1.   We must begin to do things together. This occurs on two levels. The first is the "official" level, including the many dialogue groups consisting of theologians and leaders of various traditions. The second level is the grassroots level, and of the two, it is most important insofar as it is foundational. The official dialogues consistently state that their level of discussion is useless without the grassroots level.

We can worship together, and this will be spelled out more concretely in the next section. But perhaps even more foundational is to study and talk together. If you are working through this book with a small group, then you are already involved in this step, especially if your group is making efforts to convene with members of another tradition(s).

2.   Education needs to take place in regard to intercommunion, or eucharistic sharing. At present, this is not allowed by the Roman Catholic tradition (for good reasons that were discussed in Chapter Six). Sharing the eucharist does have the advantage of helping us toward unity, and giving us a taste of the unity to come.

3.   More and more areas of ministry need to be opened up to both women and men. Many Protestant communions are ahead of us in this regard. Presbyterians, for example, emphasize lay ministry in the leadership role given to elders.

4.   We need to engage in study concerning the respective values of a celibate clergy and a married clergy. As pointed out in Chapter Four, there are values inherent in both types.

5.   We need to consider the possibilities of shared leadership at local levels. The Consultation speaks of fusing the episcopal, presbyterial, and congregational forms of church government. We have to discover the practical ways in which this could be done.

6.   At present, from an official standpoint, we do not recognize one another's ministry as being valid. This problem lies at the heart of many others.

7.   We can explore a variety of possibilities regarding a centrally located authority. The Catholic papacy, as we have mentioned, has much to contribute in this regard.

An additional area not brought up by the Consultation is shared social action. This would fit under Approach #1 as something very concrete we can do together. There is already a good deal of such activity flourishing, and the possibilities are endless.

These are some indications of the types of practical questions that have to be wrestled with during a transitional phase, a phase we are already in insofar as we are considering such questions. Many of them are underpinned by theological issues, as we have already seen.

Models of Unity   When considering unity in regard to structure, one question remains, one not addressed by the Consultation, nor adequately addressed by any of the dialogue teams. What really lies at the end of the transitional phase? What is full communion? At this point, let us sketch some "models" of what it would look like, the shape of our future unity. So that there be no misunderstanding, we will begin with three models that have already been described as inadequate.

1.   The "surrender" model. This is the model presupposed by the Catholic Church up until Vatican II. All other communions must, if true unity is to be found, surrender themselves, their identities, to and into the Roman Catholic form of Christianity. We have carefully demonstrated the inadequacy of this model, and the Catholic Church left it behind at Vatican II.

2.   The "merger" model. In this model, the goal is full and in complete agreement on all issues. In order for this to take place, each tradition must "give a little," or compromise some of its uniqueness, for the sake of a greater end, that of unity. We have carefully demonstrated the inadequacy of this model, too, and like the first model, it was given no credence by our church at Vatican II.

3. The "toleration" model. According to this model, we all exist side by side, very careful to avoid two things: first, interaction, which we must stay away from in order to avoid the second, quarrelling. The cliché "to each one's own" captures this model, which could also be termed the "stalemate" model. We cannot get anywhere, nor do we really want to or need to. While this model is clearly rejected by Vatican II, it is the easiest to fall into and unfortunately a quite popular model on all fronts.

Putting these models behind us, we can move on to consider a more appropriate model, that of "full communion" or "communion of communions." There are several possibilities in this regard.

4. The "full communion from below" model. By "below" is meant the grassroots level. Presupposed here is the principle we have thoroughly investigated of "unity amid diversity." Try to imagine, unreal as it may seem, nearly all members of all mainline churches with an attitude of openness and willingness to explore and be enriched by the beliefs of other traditions. To put it differently, everyone has embraced in some shape or form the first six steps of our method for ecumenism. There is a sense in which, assuming this, there would be genuine unity. Here ecumenism is seen as a process, and the more you and others engage in interaction and mutual understanding and growth, the more full communion is accomplished. In order to give direction to this model, the next model must be added to it.

5. The "full communion from the middle" model. "Middle" is used here for lack of a better term. According to this model, theologians and leaders from the various traditions engage in carefully structured dialogues on a wide variety of topics. There is a higher degree of sophistication present here than in the dialogue going on from below simply because there is more training and experience. This model is already in full operation, though there is always room for additional effort, sincerity, expertise, and clarity. In this book, we end up considering but five of these dialogues: it is important to remember that there are, in fact, over 50 similar dialogues now in process.

The results are, when accessible in clear form, essential in helping grassroots-level dialogue take place. And also, the results are absolutely worthless unless they are grounded by efforts toward full communion "from below." Working in tandem, the two levels achieve a marvelous degree of unity.

6.   The "full communion from above" model. By "above" is meant the magisterium of the Catholic Church in conjunction with the highest levels of authority in other traditions. In this model, the unity accomplished under models 4 and 5 is endorsed and on an official level, there is the one fold asked for by Jesus with legitimate diversity. It is analogous to a marriage ceremony: prior to the official act of marriage, there is union between the man and woman who are truly in love. But the ceremony sanctions the union and proclaims it as real and lasting. In like manner, there is already unity as models 4 and 5 reach their fullness, and it is officially sanctioned, for all to see, with model 6. Let us make some further observations about this model.

• It will, of course, not occur all at once with all other mainline traditions. One reunion will happen at a time, the earlier prospects being the Orthodox, the Lutherans, and the Anglicans. Other surprises and motivating forces may be in store, as perhaps the Orthodox and the Anglicans, who are quite close, reach this stage among themselves.

• On the one hand, model 6 cannot occur without models 4 and 5 (though 4 and 5 can occur without each other, to their detriment, and 4 and 5 can mutually occur without 6). Since the people of God are the church, it would be absurd for the hierarchy to move toward union alone since, as we have pointed out, its purpose is to serve the church.

• On the other hand, model 6 will be necessary in order to serve models 4 and 5 by way of encouragement. If 4 and 5 reach a level of fullness, 6 would be necessary to complement such fullness. If such service is lacking, it would only be understandable that 4 and 5 would die out, much as if two lovers were forced to remain apart forever, it would be understandable should their love fade.

• The hierarchy has already encouraged and officially endorsed the groundbreaking activity taking place from below and from the middle. The endorsement is found in the Decree on Ecumenism, as has already been carefully noted. And in the Constitution on the Church, it is clear that since the people are the church, we are responsible for achieving essential unity, just as the married couple is responsible for forming a substantial love between them.

• There is a certain amount of ambiguity right now regarding at what point in the process of unity, begun from the bottom up, the official endorsement and, hence, public full communion ought to take place. This hinges on that crucial phrase from the Decree on Ecumenism, the "hierarchy of truths." Relativity and latitude have to be considered in two areas: At which level of the hierarchy must agreement be reached in order for full communion to be warranted? And second, how large a majority from the respective populations of the two communions ought to endorse the full communion as a prerequisite?

In answer to the first question, imagine a triangle with the top end being very basic truths of Christianity, as expressed in our creed for example, the bottom end being the numerous and intricate subtleties of our traditions and then the full range in between. If we opt for agreement needing to take place only at the very top, we are already at that stage with several (at least) other traditions. If we opt that agreement need take place all the way down to the very bottom, then we are in essence reverting back to model #1. It will have to be somewhere in between. If that answer seems arbitrary and ambiguous, so it must be at this stage.

The Roman Catholic bishops from the United States and Germany have called for a Roman Synod on Ecumenism. Their thinking is that, given the possibilities for communion, agreement should not rest with any one or even a group of Vatican offices. They see the appropriate route of response in local bishops' conferences. Such an attitude by the bishops reflect their belief in the "sense of the church" that Vatican II ecclesiology envisioned.

Concerning the second question then, the hierarchy will look very critically at the level of popular support for reunion as reflective of the "sense of church." Both the simplest and the best way to answer this question is based on the ecclesiology of Vatican II in which the hierarchy is seen as essentially serving the people who are the church. And so, we can put the answer like this: One ought not to expect much positive action from above until there is widespread precedent for it from below. Our own task is unmistakably clear in this light.

• As far as this author can see, the only appropriate model for Christian unity is the full communion model. It can exist on different levels (models 4, 5, and 6) but in its most perfect and most excellent form, it will embrace each of these.

Unity in Worship   At the heart of the tradition we all share as Christians is the trust we have in God (faith-as-trust). While the contents of our faith, which vary from tradition to tradition, are best dealt with in dialogue with each other, our common trust is most appropriately shared in the act of worship. In our worship, we acknowledge in the proper attitude of humility that while what we think and plan and do is important, we are not the ones who finally accomplish the goal of unity. God's will and God's plan are first and foremost; we are but servants doing our part to the best of our ability. At the end of the day, we say in the words of Scripture: "We are merely servants; we have only done what is required of us" (Luke 17:10).

"Unity in worship" is placed last in this chapter (which addresses concrete things we can do toward unity) to remind us that all the work we do will amount to nothing unless it is grounded in trust in God, a trust expressed in worship. Since we work together and trust together, we must begin to worship together. What are some concrete ways in which we can express unity in worship?

1.   The Consultation recommends "covenanting" (making an agreement about) worship together. For example, a Presbyterian community might make a practical agreement or covenant to have some of its members attend a Catholic service on given Sundays, and vice-versa.

2.   The entire communities from two different traditions could covenant worship together on larger occasions, such as shared feast days (Pentecost, for example). There are, of course, certain feast days, like Christmas and Easter, in which distinct traditions have time-honored traditions of worship, and privacy is perhaps best respected on such occasions. But why not forge new traditions of worshipping together on days like Thanksgiving or the first Sunday of Advent?

3.   In conjunction with this, new forms of ecumenical worship can be initiated. These can range from a carefully formulated ecumenical liturgy to loosely structured prayer services.

4.   While there is an inestimable value in commitment to one's own worshipping community (parish), at the same time we could foster a sense of freedom to experience the worship of different congregations.

5.   Our ability to worship together will also hinge to an extent on the practical problem addressed earlier, that of mutually accepting each other's ministries as valid.

6.   We can agree on the real presence of Christ at the eucharist, but recognize that since this presence is a mystery, there can be a variety of ways to express and articulate it.

7.   Actually sharing eucharist together, as already mentioned, presents a significant problem. It is discussed carefully in the next chapter.

8.   Reception of the eucharist is given a central place in each and every Catholic liturgy. Protestant traditions which do not give it such centrality in consistent fashion may need to rethink the role of communion.

9.   Adoration of the consecrated elements in the Catholic Benediction service or simply the tabernacle as a holy place is a beautiful custom in our own tradition that ought not be lost. While it need not be duplicated by other traditions, it ought to be respected by all and shared by interested persons outside our tradition.

10.   Grounding all these suggestions is the acceptance of a plurality of forms of worship. There are many ways to authentically engage in worship, and we must combat the claim: "my way is the only way." God is mystery; every approach to God has inherent strengths, and all are ultimately limited. No one form fills all needs. God is much larger than our conception and our ways of approaching God.

QUESTIONS FOR REFLECTION AND DISCUSSION

1.   Where does the Presbyterian Church get its name?

2.   What caused the split between Lutheran Protestantism and Reformed Protestantism?

3.   At this stage in your reading, can you summarize briefly the various views on the eucharist that were held by the Reformers?

4.   What is your own reaction to the doctrine of predestination? What are the strengths and weaknesses inherent in this position?

5.   What is the doctrine of limited atonement and how is it related to predestination?

6.   How can we achieve both the goal of unity and of retaining our identity at the same time? What type of attitude is needed? How does the concept of pluralism fit in here?

7.   Do you think complete uniformity is a good idea? Would it be boring and artificial? Would Christianity itself be artificial if everyone believed exactly the same way?

8.   What would it mean to have a "communion of communions"?

9.   What are some of the concrete things we can do in our local communities in order to further the cause of unity amid diversity? Why is our role so important?

10.   Have you involved yourself in any types of social action that include members of other traditions? Why might this be a good way of getting to know other Christians?

11.   In ecumenical efforts, why is it important to foster new areas of ministry for women? How are the attitudinal barriers against ecumenism similar to the attitudinal barriers against women in ministry?

12.   Why is every type of worship necessarily incomplete?

13.   What do you think are the real prospects of getting involved in the ecumenical activities of a period of transition which would eventually lead to unity?

CHAPTER EIGHT

The
Methodist
Tradition

Methodism began as a movement of renewal within the Church of England during the mid-18th century. It took strong hold in both England and America, emerged as a new denomination within Christianity, and today it ranks as one of the largest Protestant communions in our country, second only to the Baptists. John Wesley, the founder, ranks prestigiously with Luther and Calvin as one of the fathers of the overall reform movement. Although Wesley himself was a theologian, he founded a church that gives a rather minor role to dogma. As a result, the essence of Methodism is not found in any unique beliefs—Wesley simply carried over basic Anglican formularies to his new movement. Instead, the distinctive vocation of Methodism lies in its practical approach (method) to a sincere and earnest Christian life, stressing heartfelt conversion, striving for "Christian perfection," missionary zeal, and social activism.

Because Methodists do not have to subscribe to any particular creed or statement of belief (they simply promise "loyalty to Christ"), they have an intrinsic predisposition toward ecumenism's first element, openness to other traditions. In other words, there are no strong dogmatic barriers precluding dialogue with other communions. As a result, the Methodist church has been very active in ecumenical relations, establishing dialogue with a variety of other Christian groups. Also, Dr. John Mott, a Methodist layman, was very instrumental in the World Missionary Conference (referred to in Chapter Two), in 1910, which marked the Protestant beginnings of the ecumenical movement. Keep in mind, then, that the lack of specific credal statements and central teaching authority by no means renders the Methodists tradition-less. Understanding their tradition begins, as always, with their historical roots.

We will begin our historical inquiry by considering the context within which the Wesleyan revival began. We can look to three developments that would have profoundly influenced John Wesley's outlook.

1.   The Enlightenment refers to both a cultural epoch and a particular mindset. The age of Enlightenment generally refers to eighteenth century France, England, America, and Germany. The spirit of the Enlightenment has left a permanent mark on Western civilization. In its barest form, it concludes that people can come to a complete understanding of themselves and the world solely through critical exercise of reason. Such a view signaled a profound reorientation; previously, our "control of meaning" or our mode of understanding the mysteries of human existence derived from Revelation—from a power beyond us. There was an immediacy to God's presence; God actively intervened in the affairs of people. But now, taking the lead from philosophers such as Rene Descartes (France) and John Locke (England) and scientists, such as Isaac Newton (England), a new "control of meaning" developed. The unaided intellect was discovering the natural laws by which the universe functioned. It was no longer necessary to posit a God who was involved in the affairs of the world on a day-to-day basis.

A popular view of God that emerged from the spirit of the Enlightenment was Deism. God had built and ordered the universe, to be sure, and its natural workings which people could discover through their intellectual abilities certainly reflected God's creative genius. But just as a good clockmaker constructs the intricate inner workings of the clock and then has nothing more to do with it, so God created the universe and "wound it up." It now ticks away without need of any active intervention from its maker. The idea of a personal God lost its attractiveness. Using terminology introduced in an earlier chapter, God retained transcendence but lost immanence. John Wesley would challenge such an assumption.

Since the spirit of the Enlightenment still predominates in our culture, perhaps it is best at this point to expose its basic flaw. In Chapter One we asserted that an ecumenical Christianity was needed to witness to a culture imbued with secularism. That secularism has its roots in Enlightenment thinking. A critique of the Enlightenment certainly does not question the validity of human ability to discover the natural laws of the universe. Instead, it begins with a grateful acknowledgement of the advanced discoveries made possible by Enlightenment thinking, But the critique then advances on the Enlightenment presupposition that every unknown, every mystery, will eventually be uncovered and conquered—it is just a matter of time. There exists a transcendent dimension, a spiritual realm of life, which though not accessible to scientific scrutiny, is nonetheless very real. This dimension can never be uncovered and conquered, and thus it is best called the realm of mystery in human life. Christianity—a unified Christianity—above all gives witness to the existence of this mystery. It stands convinced that opening one's life to this mystery—to God—is not an irrational move on the part of those who are uninformed and uneducated but rather a very reasonable assent that alone can provide meaning and fulfillment amid the vagaries and complexities of everyday life.

2.   In addition to reacting against the spirit of Enlightenment, Wesley also reacted against the narrow boundaries of the Church of England. As the Methodist scholar Albert Outler put it, "Over all there hung a stifling miasma of apathy and stale devotion" (quoted in Piepkorn II:535). Contributing to the stale atmosphere were dry and lax worship services, lack of genuine pastoral care among clergy, a pompous ecclesiastical structure similar to what Luther had experienced in the

Catholicism of his day, and a lot of politics superceding the real mission of the church. Because of Erastian tendencies (recall from the last chapter), the church was tied to governmental control that stifled any moves toward transformation and spontaneity. Those who would have sparked some renewal therefore tended to organize outside of the established church, as the Act of Toleration (1689) allowed them to do. Wesley, like Luther before him, began a movement of renewal intended to remain within the official church.

3.   Finally, in part because of these last two aspects, the times were intrinsically ripe for renewal. Movements of reform were springing up in various areas and Wesley essentially followed suit in England. In Germany, Lutheranism had developed somewhat of a rigid formalism. The personal experience of God that Luther stressed, gradually was lost amid the rationalism of the time—which tended to identify the Christian life with passive acceptance of certain dogmas. In this context, Philip Spener spearheaded a reform movement within Lutheranism known as Pietism, which successfully refocused on personal conversion.

Another group with similar focus were the Moravians, with whom Wesley would come into close contact. Their roots go back to John Hus, a reformer from Czechoslovakia around the turn of the fourteenth century, who might be called the first Protestant. He reacted against abuses in the Catholic Church similar to those Luther would react against a century later. In particular, he rebelled against the domination of the Czech Church by German prelates, and eventually he was tried as a heretic and sentenced to death. His followers, who came to be known as the Moravians, remained cohesive amid severe persecution and repression. Finally, in 1722, events took a positive turn for them. Count Nicholas Ludwig von Zinzendorf, a German pietist (and godson of Spener), offered them asylum at his estate, which eventually became a missionary center for such groups.

In the American colonies, a similar movement of renewal was occurring called the Great Awakening. The religious life that had been transported from Europe had ended up dry and lifeless with a real lack of spiritual vigor. From 1720 till the Revolutionary War, revival movements swept across the colonies that had a permanent effect on the history of American religon. Stressing personal conversion, men like Jonathan Edwards and George Whitefield preached revivals with phenomenal success.

It was in this context that John Wesley made his own unique contribution to Christianity, and it is to his own life that we now turn. John was born in 1703, the 15th of 18 children. Because of the large family, life was very strict and ordered. His father, Samuel Wesley, was a Pastor in the Church of England, and so John's upbringing was also very devout as well as scholarly. His character was imbued with the virtue of fortitude, and what has been described as "a constitutional incapacity to do anything half-heartedly" (Piepkorn II:536).

When John and his younger brother, Charles, entered Oxford for their advanced education, they found the amoral atmosphere most disturbing and founded the "Holy Club" with a number of friends. The group, immersed in the spirituality of the early Fathers, was dedicated to a monastic routine of prayer and fasting as well as to a social dimension that involved almsgiving and visiting those in prisons and hospitals. This group was heavily influenced by the author William Law (whom John would befriend), who wrote *A Serious Call to a Devout and Holy Life*. In his book, Law encouraged Christians to devote everything—time, money, talent—to God, and to live a life of compassion and love. Another powerful influence on the group was the Christian classic *The Imitation of Christ* by Thomas à Kempis, one of John's favorite books. Because of the "methodical" and devoted way in which this group sought spiritual perfection, they were labeled Methodists.

John and Charles both eventually became ordained Anglican priests, and they set out for America to work as missionaries among the Indians in George Oglethorpe's new colony, Georgia. On the way to America, their ship was buffeted by a raging storm and John was deeply touched by a group of people whom he saw calmly singing psalms and hymns together. As it turned out, they were Moravians, also headed for America to do missionary work. Their spirit would continue to influence him throughout his life.

John spent two troubled years in America. He had a very difficult time in his missionary work, became filled with self-doubt, and had an unhappy love affair. He returned home to England bitterly disappointed. He sought out some Moravian missionaries in London (still fascinated by his experience on the boat to America), and they helped him to revive his faith. One evening, at a meeting of a religious study group, John underwent a powerful conversion experience. While a preacher was reading some material by Martin Luther, John realized that Christ's sacrifice was for him personally. As he related, "I felt my heart strangely warmed. I felt I did trust in Christ, Christ alone for salvation; and an assurance was given me that he had taken away my sins—and saved me from the law of sin and death." This experience—termed the "Aldersgate experience" after the street address where it took place—gave him the same vital faith that he had witnessed in the Moravians. This conversion marks the beginning of Wesley's revival of Anglicanism. He began to form societies of the spiritually elite within the church, and engaged himself in a full schedule of organizing, preaching, writing, and travelling. Although established Anglican churches would not admit the new Wesleyan enthusiasts to their pulpits, many of the common people were attracted to their warm, personal message that touched hearts in an experiential way. By the time of Wesley's death in 1791, there were 80,000 members and 1,300 preachers.

From the start, Methodist preachers urged the new members to remain in communion with the Anglican church, much as Martin Luther had wanted his reforms to take place within established Catholicism. But as the movement grew, it began to develop autonomously. Methodists soon began to ask for the sacraments from the lay preachers who conducted their worship. The Anglican bishops refused to ordain the Methodist preachers, and so Wesley himself began to ordain. Wesley was an organizational genius, and the new "sect" prospered because of his skill. He dispatched missionaries to the American colonies in 1769; foremost among them was Francis Asbury, who must be given a good deal of credit for the growth of Methodism in America. Wesley perfected a system of "circuit riders," lay preachers who brought the new religion to people in isolated frontier places.

In America, Methodists began with poor and outcast people who were anxious to hear a new saving message. They had little need for the orthodox formalism of an established church with set dogmas. They needed a practical religion, one that would appeal to their lived experience, and this is precisely what Wesley provided. We will take a closer look at the exact nature of this "practical religion" in the next section. Slowly, however, the new sect or "religious society" grew into a more established church. Because of discipline and mutual support, this new denomination eventually improved its socio-economic status and gained a measure of affluence. Gradually Methodism grew into what might be called America's most characteristic church. A group with counter-establishment origins had been assimilated into the American mainstream. Many other smaller and newer American denominations have repeated the same process.

Wesleyan Practical Religion   Imagine a time when you had a very difficult decision to make, perhaps a career choice. You had an opportunity to move in a definitive direction regarding a certain career. In trying to decide whether to take the opportunity or not, you experienced a deep conflict. You wrote down all the reasons why you ought to take advantage of the opportunity. The reasons were very compelling, and on paper it looked like the optimum situation. You convinced yourself that this was the direction to take. However, another element entered the picture. Deep down inside, you didn't feel quite right about the career. You couldn't explain why, but you knew that the choice you had made felt uncomfortable. This inner urge that you couldn't articulate kept gnawing at you until you recognized that this particular opportunity simply was not the best direction to follow.

These two elements of an experience often conflict in our daily lives. We could call it a conflict between "head and heart," or between the intellectual side of our experience (the cognitive) and the emotional or felt side of our experience (the affective).

To take an example from the religious dimension, a person might experience God intellectually by demonstrating that God necessarily exists and could arrive at a vast array of theories concerning God. However, that person might have no felt experience of God at all. On the other hand, one might have profoundly intense experience of God within the "heart," but might be confused or simply uninterested when it comes to theorizing about God. Both aspects of our experience are real and quite valid, and both are part of striving for a balanced personality or a balanced spirituality.

At the very center of Wesley's revival was a recovery of the felt or affective side of his experience. He reacted against the established Anglican church because he felt that it was failing to meet people's spiritual needs on an affective level. A turning point in Wesley's life, as we saw, was witnessing how the Moravians felt the experience of peace during a storm at sea. Since the two aspects of experience need each other, it was natural that as Methodism developed, it began to structure some doctrines in regard to the new faith. But the primacy of felt experience over doctrinal explanation was the hallmark of Wesley's theology, giving it a very practical bent that still remains today.

Because of this practical bent, Wesley has been accused of being indifferent to theology—"it's what you feel that matters, not what you think." It would be better to say that Wesley developed a theology that simply gave final priority to the affective rather than the cognitive dimension.

This theology is articulated in hundreds of books and pamphlets that Wesley wrote or edited. At the heart of his theology is an idea that we have already discussed several times: the difference between faith itself and conceptualizations or articulations of faith. Faith lies deeper than its conceptualization, which will necessarily fall short. Wesley then carried this presupposition to what might be considered, at least from a Catholic viewpoint, an extreme conclusion: nearly all doctrinal formulas of established churches lie in the realm of opinion. As he put it, "orthodoxy, or right opinions, is at best a slender part of religion if it can be allowed any part at all" (quoted in Piepkorn, II:552).

In this light, it is understandable why Wesley's theology lacked a certain intellectual systematization. If the essence of Christian faith cannot ultimately be systematized, perhaps it ought to be expressed in a different mode. This different mode of expression turned out to be the hymns written by John and his brother Charles. Wesleyan theology was captured best in verse and music, and Charles remains one of the most influential hymn writers in Christianity (for example, he wrote the Christmas favorite, "Hark the Herald Angles Sing"). To be more specific, Wesleyan eucharistic theology is best understood through a collection called *Hymns on the Lord's Supper*. These hymns pave a middle road between a purely symbolic interpretation of the eucharist (Zwingli) and an extreme realism.

How does the Roman Catholic tradition compare with Methodism in regard to this "polarity" between the intellectual and the lived aspects of experience? The saints and the spiritual masters are the ones who have stressed the centrality of lived, felt experience. On the other side, our tradition has had no lack of scholars who have articulated the faith in rational terms. The rational side has certainly received much more emphasis in Catholicism than in Methodism, and our tradition would be ill at ease with Wesley's rendering of so much dogma as mere opinion (especially in light of the fact that, as we have seen, Catholicism sees ongoing tradition as a vehicle of revelation). Perhaps one of the best hints of a real balance existing within our tradition can be seen in the life of one of our greatest theologians, Saint Thomas Aquinas. He wrote one of the finest theological syntheses ever written, the *Summa Theologiae*. Yet at the end of his life, he commented that his writings were all "like straw"—compared to the lived experience of a loving God.

In the centuries following the Reformation there was great emphasis on dogma in the Catholic Church. The "scientific" mentality of the later nineteenth century and early twentieth century saw a myriad of highly rationalistic theological works appear. Vatican I (1870) can be seen as an official paradigm of this rationalistic approach. In 1879, Leo XIII's encyclical *Aeterni Patris* established the highly cognitive Thomistic philosophy as the language of the theological schools. It is important to view such tendencies in their proper context. Because of the many divisions among Christian bodies as well as the onslaught of the modern scientific age, there was an understandable need to formulate one's official position carefully with reason and logic. The Methodists and Pietists (a parallel movement within eighteenth century Lutheranism which we mentioned earlier) were reacting against this with an emphasis on "experienced" religion.

Vatican II helped Catholics rediscover this side of religious experience that touches the heart—something which has always been part of our tradition but which had been de-emphasized following Vatican I. There was a recovery of faith as heartfelt intimacy with Christ in prayer and community. We have seen many signs of this recovery: prayer groups, the Charismatic Movement, the Cursillo Movement, retreat houses, and the Marriage Encounter Movement. These movements resemble Wesley and Methodism in the carefully organized route they plot out to make Christianity vital and practical in the hearts of more or less nominal Catholics. With this common ground, Methodists and Catholics can work together in the task of finding a place for God in daily experience. "We rejoice in our mutual discoveries of significant resources in our respective traditions which aid such development, such as the sermons and spiritual directives of John Wesley and, say, the *Spiritual Exercises* of Saint Ignatius Loyola. We are convinced that as we recover and reclaim the rich mutual heritage for ourselves, we might grow closer to each other on a deeper level" (Report of the Joint Commission, 3rd series, par.30).

Another facet of Wesley's theology, closely connected to affective religious experience, also offers a strong element of convergence with Catholic thought. A primary theme in his "practical religion" was Christian perfection or sanctification, a stress on holy living. At Oxford, John and his friends had reached back into tradition and found inspiration in the writings of the early Fathers, who often stressed leading lives of perfection. With this stress, Wesley's Methodism can be seen as a reaction against certain aspects of the thought of Luther and Calvin and, as it turns out, a convergence with the Catholic position.

Part of a life of perfection for Wesley were good works. He did not want to abandon "faith alone" but rather wished to place it in dialectical tension with holy living. That is to say, faith and works are not exclusive facets but complementary facets. Perhaps his conviction that both must be part of Christian living was grounded in the two most dramatic experiences of his life, each representing one of the facets—his Oxford experience and the Aldersgate experience. It was not until he experienced that faith came first (Aldersgate), however, that his stupendous energies in the Christian cause were fully unleashed.

Against Calvin's doctrine of predestination, Wesley affirmed free will. This led him into a lifelong battle with the Calvinist branch of the Church of England. It indicates another convergence with a Catholic position.

Ecumenical relations between Methodists and Catholics are much helped by this type of convergence. There was, of course, no historic moment when Methodists separated from Catholics, as is the case with other mainline denominations. Instead, as we have seen, Methodism broke away from Anglicanism. Since there is no historic break between us, and since certain of Wesley's themes resonate so well with Catholic positions, our dialogue with the Methodists has a "head start," so to speak.

A joint commission has been set up between Methodists and Roman Catholics and has met a number of times throughout the past decade. In a closing comment of one of the commissions' reports, we find clear evidence of a genuine ecumenical spirit at work: "What is remarkable is that wherever Roman Catholic/Methodist discussion and cooperation takes place at all, the available evidence suggests that the experience is a positive one. We hear nothing of tension, frustration, and flagging interest, but much of growth in understanding and sympathy" (Growth in Understanding, par. 117).

The commission has published agreed statements on a variety of topics. Some of the topics are ones that we have dealt with already in some of the other dialogues, such as the eucharist, ministry, spirituality, and authority. Since considerable attention has already been given to these, in this chapter we will embark on a fresh theme, introduced in the following section.

Moral Decision Making   One area we have not yet considered is that of moral decision-making. We have suggested that a prerequisite to "full communion" would be substantial agreement on the upper levels of the "hierarchy of truths." Does the realm of morality fit somewhere on this hierarchy? Will substantial agreement on certain moral issues be essential for full communion?

All Christians must, of course, subscribe to Jesus' basic moral dictum, "love your neighbor as yourself." But the fact is that when it comes to applying certain universal gospel values to particular and specific moral issues—especially issues that did not exist in Jesus' time—there exists a vast pluralism of conclusions. This is especially true during times of rapid social and cultural change, as is the case today. Sincere believers, we find, hold quite different and often opposing stances on moral issues such as Capitalism and Socialism, marriage and sexuality, nuclear armaments, and a host of other issues.

Added to the complexity is the fact that official stances taken by, for example, the Roman Catholic teaching authority have developed and changed throughout the centuries. Like so many other aspects of our tradition, they are historically conditioned. For example, usury, the taking of interest on loans, was once forbidden. With the emergence of new socio-political factors, this stance was reversed. Today, we find ourselves beset with many complex moral issues that were unheard of just a century ago—in the field of bioethics, for example. It will take much time and careful examination to develop a mature perspective on such issues.

As a result of such complexity, we cannot simply delineate a Catholic stance or a Protestant stance on ethical issues and then try to imagine ways of coming to substantial agreement. Instead, we must realize that there exists a wide pluralism within each tradition regarding these issues today. Although such pluralism often leads to heated (and healthy) discussion and disagreement within a tradition, it need not cause divisiveness and generally does not cause division. Two people can be passionately committed to opposing stances on a moral issue and still have a common faith and worship together. Thus, there is no reason to think or demand that things be any different as traditions move toward fuller communion with each other.

The dialogue teams who choose to discuss this area—as the Methodist/Roman Catholic dialogue has done—will find it helpful to examine the basic process by which a Christian arrives at a moral decision. A certain unity is discovered as we recognize that we all share a similar process that involves three basic factors. Different people within different traditions will, of course, balance these factors differently in their attempt to live the gospel as authentically as possible.

1.   AUTHORITY   First, we are all members of a tradition, a community. Our churches have centuries of experience behind them, long traditions in which they have wrestled with many complex moral issues. We can consider ourselves blessed indeed to have this context within which to make our own moral decisions. By ourselves, we exist during our lifetime in only a small portion of history. Our perspective is necessarily limited. Thus, we are in need of a patterning that has emerged from a wider perspective and a longer, more varied experience. Part of this patterning consists of the teaching authorities of the various traditions (for Catholics, the magisterium) whose purpose is to serve the ultimate norm, the word of God.

2.   CONSCIENCE   Secondly, decisions that we have to make are our own decisions. We enter situations throughout our lives that are unique unto themselves. When we have a difficult decision to make, no one else has ever been in our exact circumstances. Thus, we need to look within ourselves very carefully to make the best possible decision. This aspect of our decision-making process is called conscience. It is a developed capacity within us to discern what is good and what is evil. Notice the word "developed." No one has an automatic inborn capacity to make the right decisions. This capacity is something that must grow and develop and mature within us. Different individuals will be at different stages in this

developmental process. Consider, for example, the difference between a twelve-year-old and a wise, old person with many years of experience reacting to the same situation.

These first two factors, social authority and personal conscience, must both work together in the decision-making process. As members of a particular tradition, our consciences have been deeply influenced by that tradition, and, therefore, in many matters it should be perfectly natural for us to agree with official teachings. Yet the church may have taken a stand on a particular issue in which we are personally involved, and deep within ourselves, in our conscience, we feel we must take a different stand. The most common example of this in the American Catholic Church today is the moral issue of contraception. While the magisterium has taken a definitive stand against artificial contraceptives, many consciences might dictate otherwise.

3. PASTORS AND THEOLOGIANS   Before returning again to those situations in which authority and conscience conflict, we must acknowledge an important third conflict in operation between official church authority and the individual conscience. This is especially important for Catholics to be aware of as well as those looking at the Catholic tradition from the outside. As Cardinal John Henry Newman pointed out, the individual Catholic is not left in the unenviable position of either accepting official church positions or else having to abandon the church and "go it all alone." There is a body of public opinion in the church, formed by the living tradition, current experience, the expertise of competent scholars, and the sensitivity of individual pastors. These can also lend aid and guidance to the individual's conscience alongside the official church teachings. This area of allowable freedom of judgement is necessary to relate the universal teaching authority's official statements to the ever-changing circumstances of individuals living in varied times and cultures. Sometimes this unofficial body of informed opinion can and must clash with official stands. In fact, as we have seen, official stances can change throughout history, and often it is this body of opinion that directs and guides such change. The individual, therefore,

has more than one line of ecclesial guidance and may decide in conscience that he or she must be guided by an unofficial position in a particular case.

Now let us return to those circumstances where conflict and tension do, in fact, take place between church and conscience. What ought one to do in such a situation? First of all, the individual must strive for openness. In the words of the Methodist/Roman Catholic report, "Since people have the responsibility of fostering, protecting, and following their conscience, it needs to be formed and informed and must therefore be open to guidance from authority.... The Christian is one who stands under authority" (Report of the Joint Commission, 3rd series, par.43). After one has taken the responsibility of being open to authoritative guidance, then one must freely and faithfully follow his or her own conscience, informed by the third factor explained above. As long as this process is followed at times of conflict, then one is not guilty of the ethical individualism so prevalent in our culture today: making moral decisions with no reference at all to any other authority than one's own sense of what is right and wrong.

While both Methodists and Roman Catholics can agree in regard to these factors involved in moral decision-making, there admittedly is a difference in how heavily one factor weighs in relation to the others.

> "In both our churches we are under ecclesiastical authority, but we recognize a difference in that some pronouncements of the Catholic Church are seen as requiring a higher degree of conscientious assent from Catholics than the majority of pronouncements of the responsible bodies of Methodism require of Methodists" (ibid., par.47).

In Roman Catholicism, as we have seen, there has always been a stress on a need for mediation between people and God. Thus, when a person is faced with a difficult decision, and realizes that God's help is needed, the authority of the church exists to help mediate the will of God to that person. As we have seen in previous chapters, the spirit of the Reformation placed a much greater stress on the individual in relation to God as it reacted against extreme forms of ecclesial mediation.

Today, we also find in Protestant communions, such as Methodism, a greater stress on the role of the individual's conscience in making moral decisions.

Christian Marriage   Our culture today severely challenges and often simply disregards the sanctity of marriage. It tends increasingly to ignore the vital need for marriage as the context for sexual relationship and fails to see the need for deeply rooted family life as a firm basis for a stable society. In light of this wider cultural context within which all Christian traditions exist, a united affirmation of Christian marriage is absolutely essential. Together we must cherish and support the Christian bond of marriage. The Methodist/Roman Catholic dialogue provides such affirmation: "...it is imperative that we witness together to the centrality of marriage in God's purpose for human community. Such common witness must not be seen as an attempt to hide our disagreements for the sake of ecumenical good will, but as an urgent necessity if the world at large is to be influenced at all by the ideal and practice of Christian marriage" (Growth in Understanding, par.39).

This excellent commonality among Christian communions stems from the fact that for all of us, marriage is sacramental. A sacrament, in the widest sense, is a concrete instance of the love of God touching the human condition. The fidelity expressed between partners in marriage is a beautiful sign of the faithful love God has for a troubled world (Ephesians 5:21-33). The sacramentality of marriage needs to be proclaimed by all Christians to the world.

A delicate moral problem arises, however, with the question of the permanence of marriage. While all traditions uphold the sanctity of marriage and consider the commitment to be of utmost seriousness, the fact remains that some couples within the traditions do experience severe pressures upon their marriages. These pressures are often caused by certain inescapable cultural forces that place undue burdens on the marriage. Thus, there are Christian couples who must face the prospects of separation, divorce, or remarriage. How do the various traditions face this moral problem? This is a good "case study" within which to examine the three decision-making factors (outlined in the last section) at work.

In the traditions we have been considering, the official teaching authorities certainly endorse, support, and encourage permanent marital commitment. However, they realize that there are times when in good conscience a couple may have to divorce and re-marry, and they recognize this as legitimate. For Roman Catholics, a much heavier emphasis is placed on the doctrinal tradition of the church, upheld by the magisterium, which proclaims that marriage as a sacrament is permanent regardless of the circumstances. Thus, divorce followed by remarriage would, from an official standpoint, place those involved outside the Roman Catholic communion.

Such a position causes considerable pain to faithful and loyal Catholic couples who in good conscience sincerely believe that their marriages have ended. What are their options? They certainly ought not simply suppress their conscience; after all, the Catholic tradition has always held that one ought never to go against one's conscience. Are they to go it alone or join another communion? While they are free to do that, there is a way in which they can remain reconciled to their own Catholic tradition.

The official channel endorsed by the magisterium is the annulment process. Through careful scrutiny, it may be discovered that at the time of marital commitment there existed an unforeseen impediment to true union from one or both of the partners. Now the impediment has manifested itself and the judgment is made that a full sacramental union never existed in the first place. The marriage can thus be annulled, opening the way for divorce and remarriage.

It is true that such a process follows logically from the position that genuine marriage is indissoluble. However, several problems arise. To some, such practice is too legalistic— following the letter rather than the spirit of the law. Or it may appear to be, in some cases, a purely arbitrary decision on the part of the church. Thus, there are those who do follow this route but are not granted an annulment. It is in these situations that another mode of ecclesial reconciliation seems necessary. Other options need to be spelled out in dialogue.

The primary mode of ecclesial guidance for the individual Catholic conscience, the magisterium, will necessarily move slowly, if at all, toward a modified stance. It must be remembered that the magisterium has the unenviable task of speaking universally to a variety of cultural situations that are often in constant flux. Thus the need for a mediating presence of pastors and theologians can be seen. It is also important to recall what we said about authority in Chapters Three and Four. We are moving away from the idea that there must be a clean uniformity from the top of the pyramid—the pope—on down through each individual Catholic. The principle of subsidiarity suggests that the pyramid is turned upside down. The people, in their diversity, are the church. The teaching authority serves the unity of the church by offering universal guidelines that, while undergirding the whole church, must be mediated to particular situations. This model represents the kind of consensus that our church, and eventually a unified Christianity, should strive for in the realm of morals.

Ecumenism and Intermarriage   We said in the last section that amid the differences regarding divorce and re-marriage, a unifying element is found in our common witness to the world of the permanence and sacramentality of Christian marriage. Another potentially unifying witness is the phenomenon of intermarriage. More and more frequently, people from varying traditions are falling in love and deciding to commit themselves to one another in Christian sacramental marriage.

The Methodist/Roman Catholic dialogue has an important insight to contribute in this regard. Too often we tend to see those seeking intermarriage as posing a problem for the churches involved, a problem in terms of doctrine, ecclesiastical policy, and pastoral care. But the fact is that this so-called "problem" has an underlying cause, namely, the division of our churches in the first place. The churches must look to themselves and honestly say "this is our problem, not their problem." Thus, those involved in intermarriage should be warmly welcomed. But even further, a couple seeking intermarriage who have a sincere sense of commitment to their respective traditions can be seen as involving themselves in a truly ecumenical endeavor.

First, they are a witness of a certain existing Christian unity to the world. And secondly, they are a poignant challenge to the Christian churches themselves. In a sense, they are truly "riding ahead" of the current rate of ecumenical progress. They offer a vision of the unity to come, for in a unique way, they have already embraced that unity. This is a perfect example of a theme we have emphasized throughout—Christian unity begins with the people who are the church. Let us consider some of the ramifications and challenges inherent in this very promising ecumenical phenomenon. (These have been considered in ARC Marriages. "A Study of U.S. Living Episcopal-Roman Catholic Marriages").

The churches are truly called to an "examination of conscience" upon the realization that their structures are often seen by the couples as simply getting in the way:

> Family unity based on faith in a common Lord is complicated by demands for unswerving loyalty to one's denominational requirements. An insoluble situation often results in the church being reduced to a purely organizational and administrative construct. The church seems to be the problem and, therefore, may be relegated to a very secondary role in order that the positive good of a Christian marriage may be realized (p.5).

Thus, many couples find that the only way of building a faith life together is to regretfully ignore the church discipline of the two traditions involved.

We can point to several concrete examples where church discipline causes divisiveness instead of promoting unity. These can be seen as positive challenges to the Christian traditions. First, since some traditions fail at present to recognize the validity of one another's ministry (treated in Chapter Six), problems arise from the outset as regards the marriage ceremony itself. Often there exist cumbersome requirements for matrimonial validity. How many couples have started their intermarriages with a bad flavor in their mouths for their respective traditions? And how many couples, discouraged and annoyed by the cumbersome discipline resulting from our disunity, have simply opted for non-sacramental marriage outside either tradition?

Second, the problem of intercommunion (considered in Chapter Six) sends ripples of division into intermarriages. How does the couple worship together? Must there always be included in their worship the pain of not being able to share mutually in the Lord's Supper? This is truly a challenge to the ecumenical integrity of the churches, as the sacramental sign of unity par excellence itself causes division.

Thirdly, how does all of this look from the perspective of the children? Do they sense they have been baptized into a common faith—or a denominational squabble? Are they to practice the sacramental life in one tradition (decided upon arbitrarily?), or are they to alternate between the two traditions, participating in both? When the later is chosen, then is it perhaps true that "the children have no background roots of identity and are less able to find a real spiritual home in either church"? (ARC Marriages, p.7).

All of this points to the deep pain occasioned by the lack of Christian unity. We must bear the pain, but also allow it to work within us toward conversion that leads to unity. The closing words of the Methodist/Roman Catholic dialogue capture well the need for ongoing change within all of us:

> Those who have made a start best know there is still a long road to travel, but that is not a reason for failing to start, nor yet for fainting by the way. We should always be ready for further experiment, for extending our contacts and joint concerns.
>
> Neither John Wesley and his followers nor the great apostolic figures of Catholic history were marked by a readiness for discouragement of an unwillingness to swim against the tide. It is our privilege to live in an age when we clearly see the search for unity as integral to the whole witness of Christ, and though that vision is not proof against doubts and discouragement, we should not betray the spirit of resolution and confidence which, in Christ, we have inherited from his great servant (Growth in Understanding, par. 118-119).

QUESTIONS
FOR REFLECTION AND DISCUSSION

1.   What role did "experience" play in John Wesley's life? Why do you think he assigned such a small role to doctrine?

2.   In your own life, think of some occasions in which the inner experience or inner feeling was missing. In your life as a Catholic, have there been times like this?

3.   What do you think might be the danger of relying too much on the affective dimension of religion to the neglect of carefully formulated statements of belief?

4.   Do you find yourself appreciating the strong guidance available from the teaching office of the church? Or do you find yourself reacting against it?

5.   What is your reaction to this statement: "If you don't follow the teaching of the church in all instances, you have no right to call yourself a Catholic?"

6.   How might a Methodist react to a similar statement?

7.   In regard to marriage, what message do you think our churches have to offer the world at large? Why is it especially important to focus on our similarities in this regard?

8.   Do you tend to agree or disagree with the Catholic Church's teaching on divorce and remarriage? Do you have Protestant friends who react strongly to the Catholic position?

9.   What does it mean to say that marriage is sacramental?

10.   In what ways might a healthy intermarriage act as sign of our future Christian unity?

CHAPTER NINE

The
Evangelicals

We have examined the ecumenical endeavors between our Roman Catholic tradition and the traditions of those mainline churches that descended directly from the Reformation. There remains one more Christian tradition we ought to consider. It is a cross-denominational group of Christians who are termed "Evangelicals" who have had and continue to have considerable influence on the American religious scene.

Generically speaking, an Evangelical is one who follows three basic theological principles: 1) the full authority of the Scriptures in matters of faith and practice. There are strong roots here in Luther's *sola scriptura;* no particular tradition is authoritative. 2) The necessity of conversion, that is, personal faith in Jesus Christ as Lord and Savior. The affective dimension of experience takes precedence over the cognitive dimension. 3) A sense of urgency in seeking the conversion of sinful men and women. This involves massive revival crusades that attract great numbers of people in the United States and throughout the world, as well as "one-to-one" witnessing of the gospel. Evangelicals have met with astonishing and admirable success in their goal of spreading the good news to everyone.

As in any tradition, there is a good deal of pluralism among those who call themselves Evangelicals. Different individuals put more or less focus on each of the three "common denominators" outlined. There are those who would lay the heaviest stress on the first, and thus could be termed "biblicist" Evangelicals. Those placing more stress on the second could be called "pietistic" Evangelicals. And there is a great range of diversity when it comes to the third principle. For some, conversion of individuals is what ultimately matters, while for others, social action plays a critical role.

Another factor contributing to Evangelical pluralism is its cross-denominational or non-denominational dimension. While Evangelicals can be found within any tradition—including our own—there are certain denominations that tend more than others toward an evangelical mindset. The largest group are the Baptists in their various denominational forms: the Southern Baptist Convention, the American Baptist Churches, and the National Baptist Convention. Methodists also play a role, especially the Free Methodists, and the Wesleyan Church, and the Church of the Nazarene. Finally we find what are termed "pentecostal" groups such as the Church of God, the Church of God in Christ, and the Assembly of God. Some of these groups, such as the American Baptists, have an openness to Ecumenical endeavors, while others remain strongly opposed. The non-denominational Evangelicals can tend to be somewhat bitter toward established historical traditions, convinced (often from experience) that their institutional and orthodox structures only invite complacency in regard to authentic witness to the gospel. As such, they tend to be separatist by nature.

With this brief overview, it may be obvious that Evangelicalism poses quite a challenge to Roman Catholicism in regard to establishing ecumenical relations similar to those that we have with other traditions. However, we have more in common than meets the eye, as we shall discover; there is great potential for turning our differences into sources of mutual enrichment.

The Roots of Evangelicalism   The word "evangelical" can be confusing and misleading because it has been used in a wide variety of contexts throughout the centuries. The word comes to us from the Greek *evangel* meaning "bringing good news." We have traditionally, for example, called the writer of the gospels (gospel means good news), the four evangelists, meaning those who proclaim to us, in writing, the good news of Jesus Christ.

During the Protestant Reformation, those following Luther were designated as Evangelicals or Evangelics to distinguish them from the Roman tradition and the Reformed tradition. Some Lutheran churches today still use the term as part of their official designation, and many of them tend to be unhappy with modern evangelicals using this term, causing an understandable confusion as regards their own Lutheran identity.

During the eighteenth century, we find what is called an evangelistic revival taking place on the fronts, three of which were previously described: 1) In German Lutheranism, the revival took the name of Pietism; 2) In the Church of England, the revival was Wesley's Methodist movement; and 3) In America, a movement called the Great Awakening swept across the colonies. A similar development took place in Roman Catholicism around the same time. Alphonsus Ligouri (1696-1787), founder of the Redemptorists, took the lead in Italy in spreading devotions appealing to the emotional, affective dimension of people's experience.

In early nineteenth century America there was a second "Great Awakening" in New England and a similar wave of revivals on the frontier. Like the first Great Awakening, it swept across denominational lines and influenced a pervasive evangelical undercurrent in American Protestantism. The emphasis on preaching rooted in the Bible and oriented toward individual conversion, was here to stay. The two awakenings began the phenomenon of revivalism which has had a conspicuous effect on American religion. Our greatest revivalist preachers have been George Whitefield, Charles Finney, Dwight Moody, Billy Sunday, and Billy Graham. The Catholic parallel to revivals were "missions," which were not always the relatively calm affairs of recent parish missions, but which often incorporated "fire and brimstone" appeals much like their Protestant counterparts.

During the nineteenth and early twentieth centuries, a momentous change took place in the intellectual climate, giving birth to what is called theological liberalism or modernism. In turn, this new climate would provide a completely new backdrop against which "evangelical" theology would act and react. What did this momentous change entail? The rise of psychology and sociology had the initial impact of reducing religion to a mere mental or social phenomenon: it was thought to satisfy some inner longings, or provide society with a handy means of controlling moral behavior, but its asserted ends (establishing a relationship with a personal God, providing access to heaven) were labelled illusory. The gradual rise of a new economic theory—Marxism—suggested likewise that religion was only the "opiate of the people." A new academic discipline, the comparative study of world religions, seriously questioned the uniqueness of Christianity. The awareness that a vast percentage of the world's population sincerely follows other highly developed and seemingly genuine religious faiths challenged the assertion that one must follow Jesus Christ and him alone to find salvation. New biblical studies coming from German universities called into question both the uniqueness and the historical validity of many aspects of the Judaeo-Christian heritage. Finally, the rise of Darwinian biology—the theory of evolution—appeared to shatter biblical revelation.

Against this backdrop, American Protestantism underwent a schism of sorts, from which it has never fully recovered. At issue was the perennial problem of Christianity: How ought the values of Christ, who said his followers should be "in the world but not of it," be related to culture? Simply put, this is the problem of Christ and culture, and the relationship can take three basic forms (with many shades of meaning among the three). First, Christianity can seek to accommodate itself to a cultural form. Second, Christianity can repudiate or reject the cultural form completely. Finally, Christianity can try to embrace "both horns" at once, both accepting changing cultural forms and adapting to them, while at the same time challenging those forms, acting as the "conscience" of a culture. This last stance is the most mature and most difficult.

American Protestantism in the early part of our century reacted to the prevailing cultural form in two ways. Those embracing liberalism sought to accommodate traditional Protestant Christianity to the culture. They tried to rethink traditional concepts in fresh terms. A prime example of this was the Social Gospel Movement, in which the social application of the Scriptures was emphasized. The kingdom of God could be established here on earth by people working hard at social, political, and economic reforms. This particular reaction, that of accommodation, became the mainstream of Protestant thought at the beginning of the century, insofar as it appealed to the mainline denominations. This mainstream would then flow in diverse patterns throughout the century: following the world wars, the liberal promoters of the social gospel would lose their optimism, paving the way for a more traditional approach called neo-Orthodoxy. Eventually Liberalism led into the "death-of-God" movement and secular theology as Protestant Christianity approached the radical upheaval of the 1960s.

The second way in which Protestantism reacted to the cultural tone at the turn of the century was that of rejection or repudiation. Taking the opposite tack of Liberalism and creating tremendous controversy was Fundamentalism. It would be within the crucible of the Fundamentalist controversy that what we are referring to as Evangelical Christianity would be reshaped for decades to come. Therefore, it is important to trace the roots and outgrowths of Fundamentalism. Keep in mind that Evangelical Christianity, deeply affected by Fundamentalism that repudiated culture, exists primarily alongside rather than within the mainstream of Protestantism. Since our official dialogues with Protestants are within the mainstream, it is understandable why our ecumenical relationship with the Evangelicals is in the initial stages, somewhat as people who have lived on the same block for a year begin nodding to one another.

Five "Fundamentals of the Faith"   The roots of the Fundamentalist reaction at the turn of the century are intricate and subtle, going back to certain orthodox thinkers at the beginning of the 1800s. Perhaps the easiest way to understand this phenomenon is to consider what evolved into the five "fundamentals of the faith." These were an attempt to reduce Christian faith to simple and easily understood essentials. Along with some commentary, these are 1) The verbal inspiration of the Bible. This is the belief that God told the biblical authors what to write. This view upheld the ultimate authority and authenticity of the Bible, which had been so severely challenged. Here one can see the roots of that first common denominator of the Evangelicals, the strong reliance on scriptural authority; 2) The virgin birth of Christ; 3) the bodily resurrection of Christ. These doctrines served to reinforce the existence of the supernatural and the miraculous amid human life. Modern science had tended to reduce the miraculous to mere natural phenomena, and new biblical studies had explained away the existence of things like the virgin birth and the resurrection as mere fantasy and symbolism; 4) Christ's substitutionary atonement—the belief that he died for our sins. This reinforced the notions of the essential sinfulness and depravity of humanity and that all stand in need of salvation over and against the liberal theory that humanity was good and "salvation" could be had through the right social and political programs. In addition, this insured the existence of the afterlife—Christ died to open the gates of heaven—in opposition to the liberal theory that the kingdom of God could be attained here on earth; 5) The imminent and visible second coming of Christ. In addition to reinforcing the literal interpretation of Scripture, this fundamental belief countered the liberal presupposition that history was an open-ended evolutionary process entirely in the hands of human planning and responsibility. This Fundamentalist theme has its roots in the theory of Dispensationalism developed in nineteenth century England by J.N.Darby, according to which all of history is divided into seven time periods or dispensations during which God works in distinctive ways. According to this theory, we presently would be in the sixth period—with the last—marked by the appearance of Christ—right around the corner.

Fundamentalism, then, began a development at the turn of the century that still remains today as strongly counter-cultural. Evangelicals, who as a broad group predate Fundamentalism by several centuries, resent being called Fundamentalists. Fundamentalists, in turn, are uncomfortable being identified with Evangelicals. A concrete example of this is the very real difference between Billy Graham, who would wish to be identified as an Evangelical, and Jerry Falwell, a Fundamentalist. Many people lump them together as "revivalist preachers," and this is overly simplistic. Evangelicals have tended to break away from Fundamentalism, but not so much because of the "five fundamentals," some of which actually continue to serve as a bridge between the two groups. Rather, the differences lie more in how the fundamentals are applied. Frequently, however, the public at large inadvertently confuses Fundamentalists and Evangelicals.

Characteristics of Fundamentalism   Fundamentalists tend to display a pessimism about the human situation that is inherent in Dispensationalism. This view is rooted in the more eschatological passages of the Old and New Testaments, which speak of negative events that will precede the end of time. Thus, bad social and economic conditions are a good sign, for they point to Christ's imminent return. Because this negative situation is considered essential, there is little movivation to change human events and Fundamentalism tends to downplay any genuine social consciousness. While that activity is becoming more visible through groups like the Moral Majority, it would generally be directed toward the more conservative elements of the status quo.

Fundamentalism also tends to be anti-intellectual and non-self-critical. This results from a literal interpretation of Scripture that disallows any influence from modern biblical scholarship. Fundamentalists do not accept that such scholarship can serve to strengthen, not diminish, a biblical faith. In addition, by adhering to simplistic fundamentals, the movement tends not to possess a self-critical element. A strong reliance on what is perceived as a possession of the essential truths negates any basic need to change or develop.

Along these same lines, Fundamentalism tends to reject many of the findings of modern science, especially in regard to evolutionary theory. The famous example of this is the

Scopes "monkey-trial" held in Tennessee in 1925. John Scopes, a schoolteacher, broke a state statute prohibiting the teaching of evolution in schools. His opposition, headed by William Jennings Bryan, found him guilty in a trial that brought out the worst in Fundamentalism's public image.

Finally, because of its separatist ideology, Fundamentalism tends to have little positive regard for other Christian groups. Only the Second Coming, when the wheat and chaff will be separated, will reveal the true value of the Fundamentalist as over and against other Christians. Ecumenical activity, then, is to be avoided at all costs as a compromising betrayal of the truth.

Modern-day Evangelicals have reacted to the above traits within Fundamentalism. Evangelicals to a greater or lesser degree realize the limitations of a purely separatist attitude. Yet there is indeed a spectrum of Evangelical diversity based on the degree to which they adhere to their five fundamental teachings.

At the biblicist end of this spectrum is what can be called "Establishment Evangelicalism,," which tends not to challenge established social structures, but rather stresses individual conversion. The tendency here is to blame social problems on individuals who are not committed to Christ; such problems, therefore, will only be solved by converting individuals. Thus, Billy Graham—the Establishment Evangelical par excellence—justified his trip to the Soviet Union in which he avoided any criticism of the Soviet regime. In the realm of social concern then, establishment evangelicalism retains much of the Fundamentalist attitude though it is considerably tempered and increasingly becoming more socially conscious. The same Billy Graham has become an outspoken critic of racism and the nuclear arms race.

Establishment Evangelicalism is also more open toward other Christians in an attempt to break out of the separatism of its Fundamentalist predecessors. The best sign of such openness is the existence of respectable intellectual activity such as that manifested in the periodical *Christianity Today*. However, no significant moves toward unity with other Christians have yet taken place.

There is a younger generation of experimental Evangelicals who are often termed "New Evangelicals" or the "Worldly Evangelicals" insofar as they take their cultural milieu very seriously rather than repudiating it. It is in this promising young movement of Evangelicalism that ecumenically minded Christians can find partners for dialogue.

Evangelicals within this group are more open-minded toward new discoveries in the biblical field. In addition, they have rethought the dispensational theology of their forebears, allowing for many new possibilities of genuine social concern and action. This view is manifested in such contemporary periodicals as *Sojourners*. Finally, they are much more ecumenically minded. Though not necessarily interested in organic union of the churches, they do believe that the truth can be illumined from perspectives other than their own.

Dialogue between Roman Catholics and Evangelicals is taking place on an international level through the Evangelical/Roman Catholic Dialogue on Mission (ERCDOM) and also bilateral with Pentecostals and Baptists. The Southern Baptist/Roman Catholic dialogue in the United States is extremely important since it involves the two largest Christian denominations in this country. It may be helpful to examine the basic "common denominators" of Evangelical Christianity against a Roman Catholic backdrop. It is important to keep in mind two things: 1) the diversity among Evangelicals, which will make some of the following observations "mere generalizations," and 2) the diversity within Catholicism itself; it is not, and never has been, monolithic in character.

If there is one common denominator that all Evangelicals share, it is the deep, inner, affective experience of Jesus Christ as one's personal savior. Termed a "born again" experience, it involves the presence of profound emotions or feelings about having surrendered one's life to Jesus Christ. One might find two Evangelicals from opposite ends of the spectrum disagreeing on biblical interpretation or on social action, but the inner experience of Christ is known to both of them.

Closely tied to this feature is the desire of many "born again" Christians to give witness to the experience of Christ's redemptive power in their lives. Often in this witness there appears a stark contrast between one's former life and one's new life in Christ. The deep appreciation for this new life gives Evangelicals the impetus to give witness in a variety of different settings, including social situations, churches, or on doorsteps. The large revival meeting also plays an important role here, for it is often in the presence of a dynamic preacher and surrounded by other Christians, that people experience a profoundly moving conversion.

Roman Catholic Reactions   There are several reactions to these features from a Roman Catholic perspective. To begin with, many Roman Catholics share deeply in the reality of an inner, feeling-oriented experience of God. There appears to be a genuine need for this dimension of faith as witnessed by the tremendous appeal for some Catholics of the Charismatic Renewal as well as other movements oriented toward an affective experience of God. We cannot deny the validity of such experience. However, there exists a tendency on the part of many Evangelicals to claim that the only valid approach to God is the inner "born again" experience. Other approaches may be judged valid, but it is believed one has not really experienced God unless one has been "born again." Those who have not had this experience are considered as having not yet "arrived" in regard to personal salvation. Thus, an emotional experience is equated with God's salvific action for the individual. Roman Catholic spirituality, on the other hand, would challenge this view, inasmuch as there exists a pluralism of approaches to and experiences of God. Experience is not all of one kind. Emotions can certainly play a role and a valid one at that, but no single facet of experience is of the essence in one's relationship to God.

For example, in the Roman Catholic mystical tradition there is a spirituality in which one is closest to God at moments of complete darkness and interior emptiness. For example, Saint John of the Cross, the great Spanish mystic, wrote of the "dark night of the soul." Some great spiritual writers in our tradition have in fact warned against the presence of emotions in one's experience of God. They can be misleading; or when they are authentic, they do not necessarily connote the peak of spiritual accomplishment. Saint Teresa of Avila once stated that for a spiritual advisor, she would much prefer an extremely rational and intelligent priest over one that was pietistic and affective. This question becomes important in the context of our culture which, if it makes room for religion at all, often equates religious experience with "feeling good about yourself." The many cautions within Roman Catholic tradition indicate that a strong emotional component has often been a part of Catholic piety. The saints cited did not try to eliminate it; rather, they felt the need for the balance of a sometimes dry, but prudent and rational theology. The point is that within the Roman Catholic tradition there is no necessary equation between one's emotions and the presence of God, as is frequently the case with Evangelicals. Reason is respected as an essential component of life. Consequently, Roman Catholicism would be wary of what is perceived as a lack of balance among those Evangelicals who tend to see an opposition between the cognitive and affective dimensions of faith.

Another caveat lies in the highly individualistic approach to conversion within Evangelicalism. This feature is very congenial to Americans, given the highly individualistic nature of our culture. As a result, it is hardly noticed except from a broader perspective. There is, of course, an individualistic aspect to faith in that no one can make faith decisions for another. However, faith often occurs in response to the appeal communicated by others and baptism incorporates us into a community. The Roman Catholic theologian, Karl Adam, went so far as to say that "The Holy Spirit dwells in the first place not in individuals, but in a community, the Body of Christ." Our entire Judeo-Christian tradition is based on strong communal dimension to faith. Evangelicalism often stresses the individual's responsibility and felt experience to the apparent exclusion of the communal penance. This may explain why the traditional communal dimension of Evangelicalism is prone to assert itself by identifying with the nation rather than with world-wide body of Christians. However, the younger generation of Evangelicals is critical of its predecessors' rationalist religion and is more ecumenically oriented.

Interpretation of Scripture   Another important factor for
Evangelicals is their firm reliance on Scripture as the inspired
word of God and their primary authority. Roman Catholics
can look with admiration at the profound love the Evangelical
movement has for the word of God. However, biblicist Evangelicals in particular tend to read the Scriptures with an indis-
criminate literalism that contemporary Roman Catholicism
finds unacceptable. The belief that the whole Scriptures are
literally true is generally referred to as biblical fundamentalism
(as distinguished from the obviously related movement called
Fundamentalism). This approach can take an extreme form
in which it is believed that God verbally dictated the Scriptures (as in the first of the five fundamentals). A more moderate
form maintains that God inspired rather than spoke directly
to the authors in such a way that the Bible is literally true,
word for word. It is important to note that while biblical Fundamentalists and Evangelicals believe in the inerrancy of Scripture, the newer Evangelicals prefer the term "authoritative"
to "inerrant" and do not demand so literal an approach. While
they hold the basic message of Scripture to be authoritative
for their lives, they welcome the findings of modern biblical
scholarship. Such a view influences their ecumenical-minded-
ness, since open dialogue regarding the Scriptures plays a key
role in new ecumenical developments between the churches.
    We find another close Roman Catholic parallel in regard
to the literal reading of Scripture. For centuries, the assumption in both Protestant and Roman Catholic circles was that
the Scriptures contained no error because they were inspired.
This does not mean that either Roman Catholic or Protestants
took everything in the Bible literally, just as one allows for
metaphorical language of various types in much of what one
hears or reads. However, after several generations of seeking
to convince one another on the basis of biblical texts, a curious
hardening of argumentation and withering of the imagination
took place on all sides—Roman Catholic, Lutheran, and Reformed. Controversialists argued more and more from the
"plain, literal meaning" of the texts as if they were so many
lessons in a logic book, framed to provide answers to seventeenth century quarrels between churches. The Bible had

become mixed with strongly polemical attitudes, and the idea of the "literal truth" of the Scriptures began to harden.

This had become a tradition (albeit an unauthentic one) on all sides when a threat was posed to the faith by new European developments in biblical scholarship in the late nineteenth and early twentieth centuries. The new discoveries were termed "historical criticism" or "higher criticism." This trend, and the controversy it sparked, is referred to as Modernism or Liberalism. New historical studies showed that many biblical stories were not so unique as people thought. Other ancient peoples had many of the same stories about gods and heroes long-forgotten. It became increasingly evident that the Hebrews used many of these stories, revising them when necessary to fit their own experiences of God. Two examples are the creation story in Genesis which was found to be modeled after an ancient Babylonian epic, the *Enuma Elish,* and the "flood motif" which was discovered to be quite common among Mesopotamian peoples.

Skeptics capitalized on these discoveries, using them to undermine the divine origin of the Scriptures. Among Presbyterians and other Protestants of the United States, efforts were made to "save" Christianity from these new threats by outlawing them in the seminaries. We have seen the Fundamentalist reaction. Roman Catholics responded in the same way, although because of their stress on tradition as a form of revelation, they were not so exclusively dependent on the Bible for their faith as were Protestants. Pius X officially condemned "Modernism" at the beginning of the century. While there were certain cultural currents that deserved condemnation, the potentially fruitful discoveries of the new biblical scholarship were swept under the carpet as well. For the first third of the twentieth century, they remained there. An about-face of sorts was made in 1943 by Pius XII, who in his encyclical *Divino Afflante Spiritu* allowed Roman Catholic scholars to use the new methods. At Vatican II these methods were given the positive assessment they had long deserved and the mainstream of Roman Catholic scholarship now respects, uses, and contributes to the ever-expanding field of modern biblical studies.

While Roman Catholicism accommodated itself to the methods of critical scholarship, Evangelicalism has repudiated them. Likewise, there are some Roman Catholics and Fundamentalists who believe that anything of a scholarly or critical bearing is out of place in the church. Nevertheless, modern biblical scholarship is here to stay as a vital force within the Christian churches, serving as a common base for ecumenical design.

Ecumenical Prospects   What can Roman Catholics and Evangelicals do to overcome the deadlock that exists in our ecumenical relations? Catholics can begin to appreciate the genuine zeal for the Christian faith that exists among Evangelicals. Both groups can appreciate that each of our outlooks is based on certain absolute truths from a common tradition. Evangelicals for their part need to develop a more flexible and pluralistic outlook, recognizing that there is a variety of authentic forms which Christian faith can take.

All of our goodwill, however, cannot and should not overshadow what Roman Catholics perceive as the greatest barrier to ecumenical engagement. This is the third "common denominator" considered above—giving witness to the faith or evangelizing. Catholics also wish to bear authentic witness to the Christian faith. This means, in effect, witnessing to people imbued with a secularized culture. Until very recently, the typical Roman Catholic approach was often abrupt, forceful, overbearing, hostile, proselytizing, making light of modern values and problems. The Second Vatican Council declared the church's own dissatisfaction with that approach (especially in the Constitution on the Church in the Modern World) and opted for a gentle, reasonable, open manner of invitation and dialogue—the essence of an ecumenical spirit. More and more Roman Catholics need to make this spirit their own; and we might ask Evangelicals whether they too could contemplate a similar approach.

The Evangelicals have no instrument such as a council of bishops to turn the whole body gently (or not so gently) around to a new course. But they do have dedicated, earnest, intelligent leaders like those pioneers who laid the groundwork for change in the Roman Catholic Church a generation ago. Catholicism has survived throughout the ages partly because our conservatives have not remained totally inflexible in the face of our changing culture and history. The Evangelicals can do likewise.

We can, at the present, be rightfully concerned about the somewhat ambiguous witness to Christianity that emanates from American Evangelical sources. But we must remember that the same concern is also appropriate for any large and popular Christian tradition. In order to grow gradually toward oneness and maturity, mutual dialogue and criticism are needed. If these components seem to be lacking among some Evangelicals, we can remember that the same has also been true within Roman Catholicism. A considerate attention to Evangelical Christians, such as that given Roman Catholics by ecumenical Protestants for decades, is still possible despite barriers and difficulties. Much more needs to be done in terms of exploring spiritualities, bible study, scholarly encounters, and diminishing prejudice on both sides.

QUESTIONS
FOR REFLECTION AND DISCUSSION

1.   From your experience, what impact has Evangelicalism had on the American religious scene?

2.   What personal experience have you had with revivals/ revivalism, either within Roman Catholicism or in other churches?

3.   What stance did Vatican II take regarding the question of the church's relationship to culture?

4.   Why is it appealing to deal with culture from both a liberal and fundamental perspective?

5. Many people tend to lump Evangelicals and Fundamentalists together as "revivalist preachers." What are the differences?

6. Have you experienced any of the characteristics of Fundamentalism discussed in this chapter? Share your experiences.

7. Have you experienced biases toward or stereotypes of Fundamentalism?

8. Have you read any Evangelical periodicals such as *Christianity Today* or *Sojourners*, or have you observed Evangelicals or Fundamentalists in the media? With what contemporary leaders within these movements are you familiar?

9. What experience have you had of the different stances regarding the root of social problems? Have you experienced such varied views on this issue within Roman Catholicism?

10. Do you personally identify with a more affective or rational approach to faith experience?

11. What dimensions of Evangelicalism do you find most appealing?

12. Name some Roman Catholics involved in the Evangelical movement today.

13. Share any experience you may have had with an historical, critical approach to Scripture study. How has the use of such contemporary methods been helpful to you?

14. How can Evangelicals be a positive influence on our Roman Catholic approach to Scripture?

15. What do we share most in common with Evangelicals?

16. What practical steps can you take to increase understanding between Roman Catholics and Evangelicals?

CONCLUSION

As we suggested in the first chapter, ecumenism is an invitation to stretch our minds and hearts; it is a call to broaden our horizons and enrich our tradition. It is an invitation to open ourselves to the will and invitation of God. This means launching on a pilgrimage toward a deepened Catholic identity, which embraces the commitment toward reconciliation of all who confess Jesus Christ as Lord and Savior. The simple fact is that such a journey is uncomfortable and unsettling. As we said at the outset, the churches now exist comfortably side by side, and it would be so much simpler if the gospel and our Catholic identity allowed us to remain settled where we are.

All traditions may well profit my taking to heart a beautiful example set for us recorded in the New Testament. It is an example of someone who is flexible enough to open herself to God's will instead of simply following her own desires. When Mary heard the challenge and uncomfortable call of God, she responded with an openness and willingness to let go of her priorities and be led by God: "I am the servant of the Lord; let be done unto me according to your Word" (Luke 1:38). In order for God's will to be accomplished, Mary's spirit had to be open and responsive. So do we have to be open and responsive to the pilgrimage upon which we are embarked in reconciling our divided churches.

Throughout the book we have proclaimed a vision of hope which the ecumenical movement holds out to the Catholic Church. We see that the unity we seek is a reconciliation of our diversity, without losing the spirituality and theological emphases of the gospel carried in our various traditions. We look beyond this reconciled diversity, this dialogue that seeks historical understanding and contemporary reconciliation, to the day when we can celebrate a full conciliar fellowship.

We hope that we may sometime meet in each place and worldwide in an ecumenical council that would be in continuity with that of the apostles in Jerusalem (Acts 15) and the early councils of Nicaea (325) and Chalcedon (451). In such councils the Orthodox, Roman Catholic, Evangelical, and Protestant Christians would be able to sit down together, celebrate a common eucharist, recognize one another's ordained ministries, know that they confess the same Lord Jesus Christ in the doctrine delivered once to the apostles and be able to act together to improve our world. The churches involved in dialogue recognize that this unity can only be reached in stages in which our spiritual lives, our theology, our action in the world, and our ordained ministries and structures can come into closer contact.

Some churches are proceeding toward this goal of conciliar fellowship by stages, through convenanting of congregations and churches, but most especially by common prayer, spirituality, and action in the world. Local councils of churches, national councils of churches and the World Council of Churches itself represent signs on the road towards this reconciliation. When Pope John Paul II visited the World Council of Churches on June 12, 1984, he enumerated the great progress that had been made through the collaboration of the Roman Catholic Church and the World Council of Churches and councils of churches throughout the world. He was most optimistic, recounting not only the theological dialogue that produced *Baptism, Eucharist and Ministry* and to which the papacy itself must be submitted in dialogue, but also twelve other areas of progress which we have made together on the pilgrimage toward a reunited Christian community.

Certainly the twenty years of progress since the Second Vatican Council and the leadership of Popes John, Paul, and John Paul challenge our bishops, our pastors, and ourselves to bring this worldwide leadership into every place in the Catholic community.

As we have indicated in this book, there is a mass of literature produced by theologians to be "received" within our churches. This is a spiritual and educational task for congregations. Ecumenical leadership cannot be left to the theological community and the bishops and pope. As Cardinal Willebrands made clear in an address to the Lutheran community (July 3, 1984):

> In Catholic understanding reception can be circumscribed as a process by means of which the people of God, in its differentiated structure and under the guidance of the Holy Spirit, recognize and accept new insights, new witnesses of truth and their forms of expression because they are deemed to be in the line of the Apostolic tradition and in harmony with the *sensus fidelium*—the sense of faith living in the whole people of God—of the church as a whole. Because such witness of new insights and experiences are recognized as authentic elements of apostolicity and catholicity, they basically aim at acceptance and inclusion in the living faith of the church. The decree on ecumenism of Vatican II says that divisions among Christians make it more difficult for the church to express in actual life her full catholicity in all its aspects. In its full form, reception embraces the official doctrine, its proclamation, the liturgy, the spiritual and ethical life of the faithful, as well as theology and systematic reflections about this complex reality.

Therefore, our task as laity in studying the ecumenical movement is to reach out beyond our own personal ecumenical life to the catechetical, liturgical, and spiritual lives of all Catholic Christians. In our time this entails, as our book suggests, working closely to renew the religious education materials of our church so that we begin to write our history to reflect ecumenical progress with Orthodox and Protestant Christians since the Second Vatican Council. The Catholic principle of ecumenism that states we take full responsibility for the divisions of the churches in history means that we must write our history in such a way that generations emerge who know and take this responsibility to heart. Thus the return to history and reconciliation outlined in the ecumenical style of this book will become a reality in generations to come.

Likewise, the documents produced to help reconcile our sacramental lives, especially around baptism, eucharist, marriage, and ordination, must become a part of the catechetical work of all of our young people and adults alike. New understandings of baptism, eucharist, matrimony, and ordination which hearken to the great tradition which we share with the Orthodox and which resonate with the Protestant churches with whom we are in dialogue will be necessary for our young people.

Finally, it will be important for our ministry training programs in our parishes and our religious education programs to help all of our people to have a sense of mission which embraces dialogue with other Christian people who engage in that same mission under the gospel. While we Roman Catholics have a special affinity with Anglicanism, Lutheranism, and Orthodoxy in the United States where the majority of Christians are Baptists, Methodists, Evangelical, and Reformed, we have a unique role to play in the worldwide process of reconciliation among Christians. The careful and prayerful study to which this book has brought us should be an opportunity not only to warm our hearts, but also to reach out to create opportunities for such study, prayer, and action with our fellow Christian believers.

Brother Jeffrey Gros, F.S.C.

ANNOTATED BIBLIOGRAPHY

The following is a small sampling of the many works available that contribute to the broadening of our ecumenical horizons. Certain of the books appear with an asterisk to indicate that they are highly readable "starting point" works.

I. General interest for ecumenical theology

*Abbott, Walter M., ed., *The Documents of Vatican II*. New York: Guild Press, 1966. The indispensable work for anyone interested in the contemporary Church. All references in the present book are to this particular edition. Another excellent edition is that of Austin Flannery.

Baum, Gregory. *Progress and Perspectives: The Catholic Quest for Christian Unity*. New York: Sheed and Ward, 1962.

Bea, Augustin. *The Unity of Christians*, ed. Bernard Leeming. New York: Herder and Herder, 1963. Essays by the first head of the Secretariat for the Promotion of Christian Unity.

Brinton, Crane, John Christopher and Robert Wolff, eds. *A History of Civilization*, 2 vols. Englewood Cliffs, New Jersey: Prentice-Hall, 1971. One among many standard histories of Western Civilization, helpful for viewing Christianity within a broader perspective. The units on Christianity and the Protestant Reformation are recommended.

*Brown, Raymond E. *Biblical Reflections on Crises Facing the Church*. Ramsey, New Jersey: Paulist, 1975. This and the following selection are highly recommended for viewing ecumenism from the perspective of modern biblical scholarship.

_____. *The Critical Meaning of the Bible*. Ramsey, New Jersey: Paulist, 1981.

Congar, Yves. *Ecumenism and the Future of the Church*. Chicago: Priory Press, 1967. By the "father" of Catholic ecumenism.

174   ECUMENISM: STRIVING FOR UNITY AMID DIVERSITY

Dulles, Avery. *Dimensions of the Church*. Westminister, Maryland: Newman Press, 1967. As indicated in Chapter One of the present work, a tremendous shift in ecclesiology occurred after Vatican II. Of the many scholars who have described this shift in readable fashion, Avery Dulles is especially recommended. This work and the following one are especially pertinent to ecumenism.

_____. *Models of the Church*. Garden City, New York: Doubleday, 1974. This contains a chapter on ecumenism.

Ehrenstrom, Nils, and Gunther Gassman. *Confessions in Dialogue*. Geneva: World Council of Churches, 1975. A reference text listing and summarizing the vast array of official dialogues that have taken place around the world.

Fries, Henrich and Karl Rahner. *Unity and the Churches: An Actual Possibility*. Trans. Eric and Ruth Gritsch. Ramsey, New Jersey: Paulist, 1984. Two well-known Catholic theologians reflect on taking concrete action based on the ecumenical dialogues.

Gros, Jeffrey, ed. *The Search for Visible Unity: Baptism, Eucharist, Ministry*. New York: Pilgrim Press, 1984. A survey of what the churches are doing to "receive" the Lima Statement.

*Hellwig, Monika. *Understanding Catholicism*. Ramsey, New Jersey: Paulist, 1981. In regard to the present work, some readers might want to see a chapter on Catholicism. As it stands, the Catholic tradition is presented in the midst of the other traditions. For a fuller treatment, however, this book is recommended.

Horden, William E. *A Layman's Guide to Protestant Theology*. New York: Macmillan, 1968. A readable treatment of classical and contemporary themes emanating from Protestant traditions.

*Kee, Howard Clark. *Christianity*. Niles, Illinois: Argus, 1979. A historical treatment that nicely complements and enlarges the historical sections of the present work.

Kung, Hans, ed. *The Future of Ecumenism*. Vol. 44 of Concilium. Ramsey, New Jersey: Paulist, 1969. Scholarly essays on the topic.

Kung, Hans. *The Council, Reform, and Reunion*. Trans. Cecily Hastings. New York: Sheed and Ward, 1961. A call for reform from one of the most outspoken and influential contemporary scholars.

Lange, Ernest. *And Yet It Moves: Dream and Reality of the Ecumenical Movement*. Trans. Edwin Robertson. Grand Rapids, Michigan: Eerdmans, 1979. Reflective letters from a participant on the Faith and Order Conference.

Leith, John H., ed. *Creeds of the Churches*. 3rd ed. Atlanta: John Knox Press, 1982. Described as a reader in Christian doctrine from the Bible to the present. Includes the Lima document on Baptism, Eucharist and Ministry.

Macquarie, John. *Christian Unity and Christian Diversity*. Philadelphia: Westminster, 1975. A prominent scholar's treatment of the main theme of the present work.

McCord, Peter J., ed. *Pope for All Christians*. Ramsey, New Jersey: Paulist, 1976. Essays on the question by seven authors of different traditions.

Manns, Peter, ed., with Carter Lindberg and Harry McSorley. *Luther's Ecumenical Significance: An Interconfessional Consultation*. Ramsey, New Jersey: Paulist, 1983.

Mead, Frank. *Handbook of Denominations in the United States*. Nashville, Tenn: Abingdon, 1970. A reference guide for finding one's way through the complexity of denominations. Quite detailed.

Meyer, Harding and Lukas Vischer, eds. *Growth in Agreement: Reports and Agreed Statements of Ecumenical Conversations on a World Level*. Ramsey, New Jersey: Paulist, 1984.

Miller, J. Michael. *What Are They Saying About Papal Primacy?* Ramsey, New Jersey: Paulist, 1985.

Moede, Gerald F. *Oneness in Christ. The Quest and the Questions*. Princeton, New Jersey: Minute Press, 1981. A Methodist minister reflects on the key themes of the ecumenical movement.

O'Brien, John A., ed. *Steps to Christian Unity*. Garden City, New York: Doubleday, 1964. Scholarly essays on the topic.

*Piepkorn, Arthur. *Profiles in Belief: The Religious Bodies of the United States and Canada*. 3 vols. New York: Harper & Row, 1977. A standard reference with a wealth of information. Can be consulted for more bibliographical information on the various traditions.

*Ramsey, Michael, and Leon-Joseph Svenens. *The Future of the Christian Church*. New York: Morehouse Barlow, 1970. Inspiring ecumenical essays by the Anglican Archbishop of Canterbury and the Catholic Archbishop of Malines-Brussels.

Rosten, Leo, ed. *Religions in America*. New York: Simon and Schuster, 1975. An almanac useful for "facts and figures" on the traditions.

Ryan, Thomas P. *Tales of Christian Unity*. Ramsey, New Jersey: Paulist, 1983.

*Stransky, Thomas F. and John B. Sheerin, ed. *Doing the Truth in Charity*. Ramsey, New Jersey: Paulist, 1982. Statements of Pope Paul VI, Popes John Paul I, John Paul II, and the Secretariat for Promoting Christian Unity (1964-1980).

Whalen, William J. *Separated Brethren: A Survey of Protestant, Anglican, Eastern Orthodox and Other Denominations in the United States*. Huntington, Indiana: Our Sunday Visitor, 1979. Easily readable reference guide, good sourcebook for "facts and figures."

Baptism, Eucharist and Ministry (Lima Statement). Faith and Order Paper No. 111. Geneva: World Council of Churches, 1982. Referred to at the end of Chapter Two.

Reference works. The following are recommended for further exploration of particular themes:

Decree on Ecumenism. A commentary by Thomas F. Stransky, C.S.P., Ramsey, New Jersey: Paulist, 1965.

Ecumenical Service of Prayer, the Consultation on Common Texts. Paulist, 1982. A guide for ecumenical prayer services.

New Catholic Encyclopedia. New York: McGraw-Hill, 1967.

Oxford Dictionary of the Christian Church. New York: Oxford University Press, 1974.

Sacramentum Mundi. New York: Herder and Herder, 1968. An encyclopedia of theology.

Westminster Dictionary of Church History. Philadelphia: Westminster Press, 1971.

World Christian Encyclopedia. New York: Oxford University Press, 1982.

*Periodicals. A wealth of material pertinent to Ecumenism can be found in these:

Ecumenical Review. World Council of Churches, 150 Rue de Ferney 1211 Geneva 20, Switzerland.

The Ecumenist. 545 Island Rd., Ramsey, N.J. 07446.

Journal of Ecumenical Studies. Temple Univ. 1936 N. Broad St. Philadelphia, Penn. 19122.

Mid-Stream. Theodor Herzl Foundation. 515 Park Ave. New York, N.Y. 10024.

One in Christ. Turvey Abbey. Turvey, Bedfordshire MK43 8 DC England.

Origins. National Catholic News Service. 1312 Massachusetts Ave. N.W., Washington, D.C. 20005.

II.   History of the Ecumenical Movement

Bell, G.K.A., ed. *Documents on Christian Unity.* New York: Oxford University Press, 1955.

Cavert, Samuel McCrea. *The American Churches in the Ecumenical Movement 1900-1968.* New York: Association Press, 1966. A scholarly history.

Desseaux, Jacques. *Twenty Centuries of Ecumenism.* Ramsey, New Jersey: Paulist, 1984.

Goodall, Norman. *Ecumenical Progress: A Decade of Change in the Ecumenical Movement, 1961-1971.* London: Oxford University Press, 1972.

*Minus, Paul M. *The Catholic Rediscovery of Protestantism: A History of Roman Catholic Ecumenical Pioneering.* Ramsey, New Jersey: Paulist, 1976. An excellent and highly readable source for pursuing in depth some of the content of Chapter Two in the present work.

Rouse, Ruth, and Stephen Neill, eds. *A History of the Ecumenical Movement 1517-1968*. Philadelphia: Westminster, 1970. The detailed standard history.

Tavard, George. *Two Centuries of Ecumenism*. Trans. Royce Hughes. Notre Dame: Fides, 1960. A scholarly history.

III.   Orthodox

Englert, Clement. *Catholics and Orthodox: Can They Unite?* Ramsey, New Jersey: Paulist Press, 1961. Short, readable treatment of the major issues, written prior to recent dialogues.

Every, George. *Understanding Eastern Christianity*. London: SCM (available from Oxford University Press, New York) 1980.

*Finn, Edward, S.J. *Brothers East and West*. Collegeville, Minnesota: Liturgical Press, 1975. This can be profitably read along with Chapter Three. Short and readable.

————. *These Are My Rites*. Collegeville, Minnesota: Liturgical Press, 1980.

Hopko, Thomas. *The Orthodox Faith. An Elementary Handbook on the Orthodox Church*. 4 vols. New York: The Department of Religious Education of the Orthodox Church of America, 1971. On the doctrine, worship, spirituality, church history, and biblical perspectives of the Orthodox.

*Kilmartin, Edward. *Toward Reunion: The Orthodox and Roman Catholic Churches*. Ramsey, New Jersey: Paulist, 1979. Excellent up-to-date resource on recent dialogues.

Meyendorff, John. *Orthodoxy and Catholicity*. New York: Sheed and Ward, 1966. A scholarly treatment.

Sayegh, Maximos, ed. *The Eastern Churches and Catholic Unity*. New York: Herder and Herder, 1963. Essays from the Eastern perspective.

IV.   Lutheran

*Bainton, Roland. *Here I Stand*. Nashville: Abingdon, 1950. A biography of Luther.

Brown, Raymond, Karl Donfriend and John Reumann, eds. *Peter in the New Testament*. Minneapolis: Augsburg, 1973. Scholarly exegetical treatment of the papacy from a New Testament perspective.

Burgess, Joseph, ed. *The Role of the Augsburg Confession*. Ramsey, New Jersey: Paulist, 1980. Scholarly essays on the question of Catholic recognition of the basic Lutheran statement of doctrine.

*Burgess, Joseph A., and George H. Tavard. *Studies for Lutheran/ Catholic Dialogue*. Minneapolis: Augsburg, 1980. A summary of the dialogues. Highly recommended as a complement to Chapter Four of the present work.

Empie, Paul C., and T. Austin Murphy, eds. *Lutherans and Catholics in Dialogue 1-7*. Minneapolis: Augsburg, 1965-1985. The dialogues themselves.

LaFontaine, Charles and Glenn C. Stone. *Exploring the Faith We Share: A Discussion Guide for Lutherans and Roman Catholics*. Ramsey, New Jersey: Paulist Press, 1980. For small groups. Recommended as a complement to Chapter Four.

Marty, Myron A. *Lutherans and Roman Catholicism: The Changing Conflict: 1917-1963*. Notre Dame: University of Notre Dame Press, 1968. Scholarly treatment of the key issues.

Olivier, Daniel. *The Trial of Luther*. St. Louis: Concordia, 1979. Centering on the dramatic years 1517-1521.

*Tappert, Theodore G. *The Book of Concord: The Confessions of the Evangelical Lutheran Church*. Philadelphia: Fortress, 1959. Has text of Augsburg Confession.

Tavard, George. *Justification: An Ecumenical Study*. Ramsey, New Jersey: Paulist, 1983. By a leading Roman Catholic participant in the dialogue.

Todd, John. *Martin Luther*. Westminster, Maryland: Newman Press, 1964. A biographical study.

V.   Anglican

Albright, Raymond W. *A History of the Protestant Episcopal Church*. New York: Macmillan, 1964.

Edeo/Nadeo. *ARC Marriages. A Study of U.S. Episcopal/Roman Catholic Marriages.* 1981. Study material was researched, developed and written by a Joint Standing Committee of the Episcopal Diocesan Ecumenical Officers (EDEO) and the National Association of Diocesan Ecumenical Officers (NADEO).

Hale, Robert. *Canterbury and Rome: Sister Churches.* Ramsey, New Jersey: Paulist, 1982. A reflection on the theme of reunion amid diversity.

*Mullay, Lawrence, and John Osgood. *A Call to Communion: Documents of the International Anglican/Roman Catholic Dialogue, 1966-1977,* with study guides. Garrison, New York: The Graymoor Ecumenical Institute, 1979. For study groups.

Neill, Stephen. *Anglicanism.* New York: Oxford University Press, 1978. Scholarly treatment focusing on the "comprehensiveness" of Anglicanism.

*Ryan, Herbert J. and Robert Wright. *Episcopalians and Roman Catholics: Can They Ever Get Together?* Denville, New Jersey: Dimension Books, 1972. Readable essays on a variety of themes.

Williamson, William B. *A Handbook for Episcopalians.* New York: Morehouse-Barlow, 1961.

Wright, J. Robert, ed. *A Communion of Communions.* New York: Seabury, 1979. Recent Documentation of Anglican reunion efforts.

The Final Report. Anglican-Roman Catholic International Commission. Washington, D.C.: U.S. Catholic Conference, 1982. Referred to in Chapter Six.

VI.   Presbyterian

*Harsanyi, Andrew and Ernest Unterkoefler, eds. *The Unity We Seek: A Statement by the Roman Catholic/Presbyterian-Reformed Consultation.* Ramsey, New Jersey: Paulist Press, 1977. Much of Chapter Five in the present work is based around this statement.

McNeill, John T. *The History and Character of Calvanism.* New York: Oxford University Press, 1954. A detailed, scholarly history.

McNeill, John T. and James H. Nichols. *Ecumenical Testimony: The Concern for Unity Within the Reformed and Presbyterian Churches.* Philadelphia: Westminster, 1974. Detailed study of the topic.

Loetscher, Lefferts A. *A Brief History of the Presbyterians*. 4th ed. Philadelphia: Westminster, 1983.

VII.   Methodism

Ayling, Stanley. *John Wesley*. Nashville: Abingdon, 1979. Recent scholarly biography.

Davies, Rupert E. *Methodism*. Baltimore: Penguin Books, 1963. Scholarly account.

Ferguson, Charles W. *Organizing to Beat the Devil*. Garden City, New York: Doubleday, 1971.

Outler, Albert C. *John Wesley*. New York: Oxford University Press, 1964. Includes his principal works.

_____. *Methodist Observer at Vatican II*. Westminster: Maryland. Newman, 1967. Observations on the Council from a prominent Methodist scholar.

*Reports of the Joint Commission Between the Roman Catholic and World Methodist Council. Lake Junaluska, North Carolina.